A WORK IN PROGRESS

A WORK IN PROGRESS

A MEMOIR

CONNOR FRANTA

Keywords PRESS

—

ATRIA

NEW YORK • LONDON • TORONTO • SYDNEY • NEW DELHI

ATRIA PAPERBACK

An Imprint of Simon & Schuster, Inc.
1230 Avenue of the Americas
New York, NY 10020

First Keywords Press/**ATRIA** PAPERBACK edition April 2015

Keywords Press/**ATRIA** PAPERBACK colophons are trademarks of
Simon & Schuster, Inc.

For information about special discounts for bulk purchases,
please contact Simon & Schuster Special Sales at 1-866-506-1949
or business@simonandschuster.com.

The Simon & Schuster Speakers Bureau can bring authors to your
live event. For more information or to book an event, contact the
Simon & Schuster Speakers Bureau at 1-866-248-3049 or visit our
website at www.simonspeakers.com.

Interior design by Dana Sloan

Manufactured in the United States of America

10 9 8 7 6 5 4 3 2

Library of Congress Cataloging-in-Publication Data is available.

ISBN 978-1-4767-9161-6
ISBN 978-1-4767-9162-3 (ebook)

For the deep thinkers, big dreamers,

and innovative creators of the world who inspire me.

Contents

In Retrospect

I'M SIX YEARS OLD. IT'S a chilly autumn day, with dew still clinging to the grass, a slight breeze in the air—and a lot of people screaming wildly behind me. The street where I stand is buzzing with athletes of all shapes and sizes, dashing for the finish line, cheered on, and, let's face it, semiharassed by spectators (though some of the five hundred runners are, to be fair, out of breath and nearly on all fours).

In our family, this day in late September is as eagerly anticipated as Christmas. That's because my parents, Cheryl and Peter, are the proud organizers of the annual Applefest Scenic 5K Run/Walk, a popular event on the social calendar of La Crescent, Minnesota, up there with the County Fair, Autumn Parade, and many other shamelessly festive small-town events. It's "scenic" because of the hilly course and golden leaves; it's an "applefest" because my home city is regarded as the state's apple capital. Yes, our apples are the shit, and we carry that prestigious title with the utmost pride.

But the point of this story is not apples. The point is that I'm bored and couldn't care less about all of these sweaty humans speed-walking toward an achievement that most of them will brag about to friends while eating a third doughnut. I prefer to create my own distractions and diversions, which is why my curiosity latches onto the video camera my dad has set up near the finish line to record every second of the madness unfolding on race day. Dad seems forever interested in documenting the things going on in our life. "Home movies," he calls them. Every occasion—birthdays, Christmas morning, athletic competitions, and school plays—is captured for posterity, as if he doesn't want to miss a thing. Maybe this explains why I'm mesmerized by this magical box with a blinking red light at the front. You know, like father like son, right?

Usually the camera is glued to his hand, with the strap wrapped around his knuckles. Or sometimes, like today, he'll leave this bulky piece of technology on a tripod, letting it run until the tape is out. When I say "bulky," I mean BULKY. This thing looks like a freaking toaster with a telescope attached. But it's the latest and greatest gadget with matchbox-sized tapes and 2-pixel quality to boot. Wow, what a time to be alive!

I know that I shouldn't interfere with his filming, but the urge is too great. I take a shifty look around: a pack of runners is bolting down the slope of Northridge—both the race's biggest hill and final stretch; nearby, Mom is in the midst of a crowd, wearing a permanent smile on her face that hides the stress of organizing such an event, and Dad, unable to stand still for more than two seconds, flits from one runner to the next, issuing hearty congratulations, sarcastic humor, and the occasional medical advice. (He's a doctor.) Yup, these two pillars of the community are more than preoccupied.

I stand on my tiptoes to peek at what is being recorded, and let

me tell you, it wasn't anything anyone was going to enjoy watching any time soon, though it could potentially be used as a good sleep aid (or a near-coma slumber). So with me being a little attention seeker, I decide to spice things up a little by putting on a spontaneous show for the future audience at home. By "audience," I mean my family. And by "show," I mean me talking about nothing for an extended period of time under the assumption that I am funny.

Nothing has changed since then.

I step in front of the camera and begin talking, making it up as I go along. I chat away as if the lens is a person, knowing that it will eventually become a person—an expectant person in my living room, gathered around to see whoever finishes the road race in record time. Instead, when the footage is transferred to the TV—via three different-colored wires connected to the recording device—they will see me goofing off and making some truly brilliant, off-the-cuff, meandering commentary on the snooze-fest unfolding behind me.

I convince myself that I am the far more entertaining option and that everyone will thank me for such an impromptu performance. But that's the annoying thing about childhood—and actually the rest of life: reality rarely lives up to high expectations.

I can't say my parents were overly impressed by my unedited act of spontaneity. Nor did I receive thanks for showing initiative.

Not an accurate portrayal of Minnesota nice, Mom and Dad!

But that, my friends, is where it all began. At the age of six. Standing near a finish line when left to my own devices. Talking into a camera.

◆ ◆ ◆

SIXTEEN YEARS LATER, here I am, writing a book, the happy consequence of talking into a camera. Thanks, Dad!

"Writing a book"—I'm saying that out loud as the words hit the page.

Man, that sounds difficult—and a little daunting, especially when I'm only a few sentences into the experience. But, regardless, here we go.

I'm twenty-two years old, and the fact that I'm writing a book feels nothing short of insane to me. Insane, but consistent with the way my life has been panning out of late.

In short, I'm a small-town kid from the Midwest who lived a relatively average life for a majority of my years. Until that day in August 2010 when I stumbled across a little website called YouTube and posted my first video, when no one was looking and no one was interested. Then life got a little weird. Hell, who am I kidding? It got really weird, really quickly.

Four years later, having transitioned from boy to man and from obscurity to something I'm still trying to define, I sit here with millions of subscribers who are, for some reason, captivated by what I'm interested in, what I'm doing, and ultimately what I have to say. One minute I'm talking to myself; the next, I'm talking to more than 4 million people . . . and that number is growing by the thousands every single day. *gets nervous at the thought and internally freaks out*

Out of nowhere, I have an audience that my dad's home videos would envy—an audience equal to well over half the population of Minnesota, and bigger than North and South Dakota combined, then doubled.

Like I said, life has gotten weird.

I am what the mainstream media refer to as a "YouTuber." I view myself more vaguely as a content creator using an exciting new platform. People like me beam ourselves into the homes of a younger generation in the same way TV stars did in the 1950s. Back then, I'm sure the older generation—so used to the intimacy, format, and familiarity of radio—was equally baffled at seeing people on a fuzzy black-and-white screen—in just the way that I'm sure there's a generation of adults out there perplexed by this whole YouTube phenomenon.

It represents the democracy of new media, where people like me can devise, launch, and maintain their own channels—and audiences—via the Internet. Look at them as mini–television shows that fit in your pocket.

What I love about the community I have built is the fact that I can connect with each and every one of them whenever I want, and then interact with them via Twitter, Instagram, Facebook, or Tumblr. We're in one big social media room together.

This channel is mine. *Don't touch it.*

But really, why does anyone write a blog or upload a vlog? Because they want to share, offer an opinion, vent, provoke thought or, if they're like me in 2010, simply bored and have nothing better to do.

But the first four reasons are my motivation for sitting down—or pacing around my apartment like a crazy person—to write this book: to expand on the page what I have touched on in many vlogs over the years. To share the challenges I've faced in my twenty-two years on earth—some universal, some intensely personal—and hope that they can comfort you, guide you, or just make you feel less alone with your own challenges.

I think I've lived quite the unorthodox life so far, but you probably feel that way about yourself too. So much goes untold in our lives. And although I seemingly live mine on the Internet, there's a lot that people don't know. I mean, why would you?

Let's visit the subject of math for a moment—adored by some, hated by me. The window on my world has so far been limited to 5 minutes every Monday. That's 5 minutes out of the 10,080 minutes available in any week; that means I've shared a little under 18 hours, give or take, talking with my subscribers between 2010 and

2014. In other words, I have only scratched the surface of what I want to share with you. And even then, the information has been posted in a well-edited, polished video. I can make a mistake, rewind, and start all over—and I can do that a ridiculously large number of times until I'm happy with how my words are delivered.

Real life isn't like that. It's one take, unedited, imperfect, and littered with mistakes that we must repeat until we get it right—a truth for teenagers and adults alike.

A computer screen mimics a TV in that it creates the appearance of a perfect life—or, should I say, "the illusion." Not unlike a selfie on Instagram or a well-crafted tweet, the computer screen projects the image I choose to portray. We all do it. My life—the glimpse obtained through YouTube—is no more perfect than yours. I'm no different. I've struggled with things as monumental as depression and my sexuality and as common as friendship, change, and body image. Some call it growing up. I call it life, and in my experience, it doesn't necessarily get easier over the years. But the eternal struggle is beautiful, and I'm happy to persevere.

In the following pages, I go beyond those 5 minutes a week that I normally share in a video. I'm going to invite you in a little further the way you do with a friend or with people you know will understand. I hope you'll be entertained, enlightened, inspired, and/or stirred. I hope I'll provoke laughter, tears, and everything in between. You'll hear some funny stories from my past, read a few words of advice regarding difficult times, and see many of the photographs I took along the way.

So here's to writing something deeper and richer than 140 characters. Here's to writing this book. Here's to us.

"So, what do you do?"

LIFE AS A YOUTUBER CAN be difficult to explain in a world still trying to grasp that, yes, content creators such as myself are carving out a living, and, no, YouTube isn't solely a place for kids with cameras to play karaoke or pranks; nor is it only a medium for adults to post clips of cute babies and cats in hopes they'll go viral.

Socially, the whole explaining-what-I-do conversation can be fun, slightly maddening, or just plain awkward. And it tends to go something like this:

PICTURE THE SCENE: *I'm at a party in a crowded room in Los Angeles (which it usually is these days). I'm happily mingling and networking when I introduce myself to some well-intentioned stranger who has no idea who I am.*

STRANGER:
So, Connor, what do you do?

This is, without doubt, the first question everyone asks in LA, to determine what brought you to this star-studded madness, how suc-

cessful you might be, and, in some cases, if you are worth knowing for longer than the next two minutes. My fixed smile doesn't let on that the voice inside my head has started to scream because I know where this is ultimately headed: the dreaded YouTube Conversation. Nevertheless, I make a valiant attempt to completely avoid bringing it up whatsoever.

ME:

You know, this and that. I'm a blogger/
videographer.

I tend to change the description of what I do every single time; it's all part of the ongoing search to find a response that will deter further curiosity, finding the one catchall label that describes what I do.

STRANGER:

Really? What do you blog about?

ME:

Oh, anything and everything. Lifestyle
stuff.

STRANGER:

Interesting. Who for?

There's no avoiding it now. In my experience with conversations like this, my career is the main thing people have trouble comprehending.

ME:

YouTube. I'm a, uh, YouTuber.

I can almost see the confusion behind the puzzled frown that greets this reply—the thought that probably goes like this: "YouTube? Like the video website? What do you do there exactly??"

ME:

I'm a vlogger, which means a blogger in video form.

STRANGER:

So you . . . you basically speak into a camera . . . in your spare time?

ME:

No, I actually do this for a living.

STRANGER:

It's your JOB??!

ME:

Yeah, I make YouTube videos. They're usually five-minute comedy skits or simple commentaries about my life in general.

STRANGER:

Really?

ME:

Yup.

What the person is bursting to say, but usually doesn't, is, "You're messing with me, right? That can't actually be a thing." But instead, the incredulity grows into hungry curiosity.

STRANGER:

And you make *money* off of this?

ME:

I do.

Feeling more and more uncomfortable now.

ME:

Well, how much do you make?

This is something people feel free to ask me all the time. Etiquette tends to go out of the window with incomprehension; the world of YouTube is so far left field that most people over thirty want to try to make sense of it all, even down to the income factor.

ME:

I make a healthy living.

STRANGER:

But . . . how??

ME:

Ad revenue. Sponsorship. The same way television networks earn money.

STRANGER:

Can I do it? You know, upload videos and make money?

The penny drops, and the stranger finally makes explicit what has only been implied up to this point: that it must be easy, that being a You-Tuber can't require much effort. Right? I mean, how hard can it beeeee?!

ME:

Well, anyone can go on YouTube. There are about three hundred hours of video uploaded to the site every minute. But it's taken me four years, four hundred videos, and a lot of hard work and perseverance to get here. It's not quite automatic success, but . . .

STRANGER:

Oh. (*Disappointment on his face.*) Well, good talking to you, Connor.

END SCENE

Usually the stranger cuts our chat short, doubtless to go home and ask his or her teenage son or daughter for a crash course on what the "YouTube generation" is all about.

So, yes, for the uninitiated, this is who I am and what I do.

But how I got here is a whole other story.

Meet the Family

IF YOU OWN AN ACRE of land in Minnesota, chances are that you have inherited or grown an apple tree. Just so we're clear, this is not an apple tree on the opposite page. It's a family tree. I grew it—sorry, drew it—for this book, if for no other reason than to illustrate the old saying that the apple does not fall far from the tree.

MOM:
Born to run, love, and care.
Stay-at-home mom. Holds down the
fort and keeps us all in order.
Sweet, kind, and compassionate.
Without her, our family would be
lost.

DAD:
Born to run, love, and
care. Works as a doctor.
One of the smartest and
most patient people I
know. Always laughing.
Big prankster. Likes to
work things out, including
people. Such a goof.

DUSTIN:
The eldest and cleverest of
the Franta kids. Old soul with
a master's in English and
literature. He should be writing
this book! Loves to run. Deep
thinker. Hard worker. Plays a
mean game of cribbage and Mario
Kart.

NICOLA:
Can do more pull-ups than the
average guy. Brilliant chef
too. Makes a better cake than
half the people on the Food
Network. Contagious laugh.
Amazing smile.

ME:
Spends far too much time on
the Internet. Cat lover. Coffee
addict. Design freak with mad
attention to detail. Deep
thinker. Friend. Lover. Hugger.
Holds self to a high standard.

BRANDON:
The youngest or, as we like
to call him, "The Angel."
Bighearted. Happy-go-lucky.
Volunteer worker. Huge
humanitarian spirit. Will one
day save the world and find
the cure for cancer. Makes
the nicest person you know
look like a total asshole.

The Good Ol' Days

The STORY OF MY LIFE starts not in Minnesota but the Kingdom of Tonga.

I'm willing to bet an arm and a leg that I've grabbed your attention now.

Yes, Tonga—that little-known chain of 176 islands spanning a 500-mile swath of the South Pacific, somewhere between New Zealand and Hawaii. Population: around 105,000. Climate: tropical. Government: constitutional monarchy. Think rugged, lush green landscapes; deep, mysterious caves; and white, sandy beaches along a shoreline dotted with harbors, yachts, and fishing boats lolling in the water. Get the picture? Google paints it real pretty, right?

Only around 40 of the 176 islands are inhabited. I know this not only because of glorious Google but because my parents lived on two of them, separately. They have somewhat of a fairy-tale love story— very unconventional, to say the least. I like to think destiny had a sense of humor when she brought Cheryl, from Montana, and Peter,

from Minnesota, together in the middle of nowhere as volunteers for the Peace Corps between 1983 and 1984.

After being stuck on an island for so long—going on runs together, exploring the caves, killing freakishly large insects, and, well, taking in everything the Tongan culture had to offer—they fell in love, and the rest is history. At one point, they were sent to different islands, meaning they had to write love letters to each other. Like, long, handwritten love letters. Sent by mail. Which meant waiting around forty-eight hours to receive a simple reply. TRAGGGIC! How did they stand it? Can you even imagine doing that with a text nowadays? Ew, no. I could never. Oh, the agony.

But as they looked ahead and faced returning to the United States, my mom wanted to be sure that beyond the Tongan love story, they had a future. She wasn't going to let my dad get away, so she moved to Minnesota. They married on June 22, 1985, not long after their return.

But enough about my Tarzan and Jane parents. This is where I come in. Fast-forward seven years later, to when I arrived in the world, though my story is less exotic and a lot more chaotic.

My home town of La Crescent is nothing special. Population: 4,500. Climate: interchangeable between very hot and very cold. Two gas stations, a pizza place, a couple of shops, and a school or two. The community that neighbors mine is the city of La Crosse in Wisconsin, situated on the other side of the Mississippi River, which acts as the state border. My charming home town, which sits beneath an expanse of rolling bluffs just south of Lake Onalaska, is pretty sedate, with people apparently as friendly as the Tongans. "Minnesota nice" is a real thing. My town earned its name because way back, land-

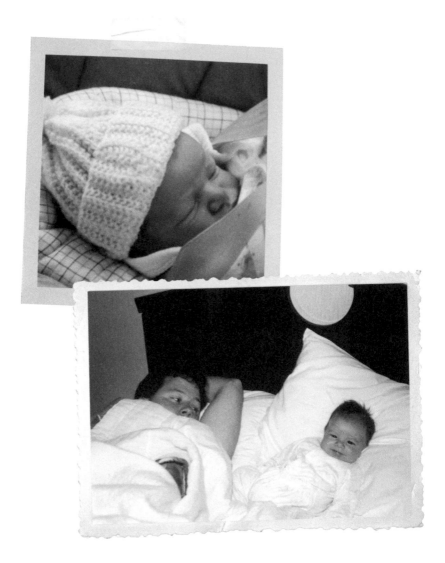

owners wanted something "romantic sounding" to attract the set-tlers (2015 update: it didn't work). Locals apparently saw the crescent shape that the Mississippi formed, and that's how it got the name. Or so the story goes. Everything aside, it's all I've ever known, and I loved growing up there.

My childhood home was a large, light-blue, two-story house with a big front yard to play in. I shared a bedroom with my little brother, while the others had their own. What a rip-off! We didn't have a big TV or video game console growing up, so we spent most of our time outdoors. We lived on a big hill at the north end of town—where there wasn't as much to do as at the south end—so we fre-

quently rode our bikes to a nearby playground or pool—hell, even a parking lot would do! Regardless of where we went, the scenery never changed: small houses as far as the eye could see, with green yards and tons of sick trees to climb.

When I think back to those days, all I can smell is Mom's exceptional home-cooked meals, which she seemed to spend half the day preparing. Oh, the smells that those works of art produced! I can also recall how meticulous and orderly everything was at home (it still is—MOM, PUT DOWN THE VACUUM!!). She kept the place sooooo clean and tidy that you could literally eat dinner right off the floor. No joke, you really could (and I probably did once or twice during my chubby preteen years).

While we're on the topic of her amazing meals, let's *talk* about her amazing meals. My mom was a traditional stay-at-home mother and cooked meals for her family five to seven nights a week. And boy, did I love that. She cooked everything from cheesy broccoli casserole with a bread-crumb topping to baked salmon with lemon sauce and crispy asparagus. Other family favorites were white chicken chili, spinach and walnut pasta, and every baked good you can think of. Ugh, now I'm hungry. Thanks, Mom.

While she held down the fort, my dad was off being the hero of our little town. He's the local doctor, and nearly everyone in La Crescent is his patient; he's truly a celebrity in his own way. Like me, he's a gadget enthusiast, although he often doesn't know how to operate the latest devices initially. One time, while sitting in front of his laptop with the blankest of stares on his face, he looked up and asked me, "Hey, Con. How do I copy and paste on this thing??" I nearly cried myself to sleep. Not, but really, beyond his inability to comprehend Apple products and social media, he remains one of the smartest people I know.

And I'll say this: Dustin, Nicola, Brandon, and I are lucky to have parents who have supported us every step of the way. I could go on and on about my amazing family, but, hey, this book is about me. So back to me.

My siblings and I thrived in our innocence by living life one game of tag and one peanut butter and jelly sandwich at a time. Take me back to those days. I loved everything, from going to the local swimming pool with friends in the hot summers, to staying up late and playing flashlight tag under the stars.

I actually spent half my childhood hanging around the YMCA and its swimming pool in La Crosse, a brick building that could easily be mistaken for an old prison. (Just kidding, but at times, it appeared like that to me.) We'd all pile in the car at 6:00 a.m. and, as a small child, I'd be left to play in the YMCA supervised play area while my parents joined friends on a 10-mile run. Parenthood didn't get in the way of their marathon training. I commend that.

When I turned nine, Mom signed me up for the La Crosse Area YMCA Swim Team. I swear she did this during my chubby phase so that I could lose a few pounds, but I took to swimming like a duck to water and I attended swim practice for the next ten years. Basically, the YMCA was my second home. If I couldn't be found at the house, I'd be in the pool, doing lap after lap, practicing for the big future I thought I'd have as an athlete. It was where I learned to interact socially from a young age. It was in that environment, more than school, that I felt less shy.

Memories of childhood: Mom's cooking and the YMCA. Oh yes,

and summers at the family cabin on White Earth Lake in Minnesota (basically, borderline Canada). Every summer, we'd drive eight hours north to stay in an old log cabin that had been handed down through the generations. We'd fish, hike in the woods, run down gravel roads, swim in the crystal-clear lake, picnic by the water, and sit around the campfire several nights a week. They were idyllic times, filled with togetherness—and lots of mosquitoes. Those were the days when people spent more time together as a family. We had electricity in the cabin but no TV or Internet. No smartphones or iPads to get in the way of bonding time.

I look back on my childhood and everything feels homely: the house, the YMCA, the log cabin. If I've learned anything in retrospect, it's that family and home are the bedrock of everything we've gone on to do. It's our base camp. Our refuge. Our only place in the world where we feel completely safe and wholeheartedly ourselves. Home, and Minnesota, is the seat of many fantastic memories that I hold near and dear to my heart.

But if you really want to find out what I was like as a child, there are only two people to ask.

How my mom is nice
When she talks
When she works
When she is cool
When she plays
When she helps me with my homework
When she is at other peoples' houses
When she is gone
When other people are over
When she goes to church
When she is in the car
When she is alone
When she is singing
When she is reading
When she kisses
When she is cleaning
When she eats
When she is yelling
When she is dancing
When she is running
When she is shopping
Love,
Connor

Letters from my Parents

OKAY, PREPARE YOURSELF. I'M ABOUT to do the unthinkable and hand the pen over to my parents. Yes, the people who created, raised, and essentially shaped me into who I am today; the people that know all my secrets and aren't afraid to blab them to each and every one of their friends in a phone call while on their way to work or the grocery store.

I already regret letting this happen. As a child, most of us dread the thought of having our parents opening up about us to ANYONE.

"Please, anything but that! I'll do whatever chore you want me to! Just, please, don't talk to my friends about that one time when I was four. IT WAS YEARS AGO. LET. IT. GO." And yet, if you are to know a little more about me, this part of the book is a necessary step. So this is what my uncensored parents thought of me as a child. The floor is yours, Mom and Dad.

Dear Connor,

As a baby, you giggled and smiled a great deal, lapping up the attention from everyone and anyone, whether we were at home or in the street. I think you liked the limelight even then. Singing and playing with you brought a smile to your face that melted my heart.

You were particularly verbal from a young age. I remember the time you said the word "stupid" . . . aged 23 months. Once, when you had learned a few phrases, and after we had put you in a time-out, you said "Settle down, Mom!"—your way of telling us that you had calmed down and were ready to be released from the time-out. Speaking your mind and expressing your thoughts came easy!

Looking back, you were always independent, determined to stand on your own two feet in the world. At 18 months, you wanted to feed yourself and walk without help. Everything was done fast, too. "Fast" is your natural speed. Be it a chore or a school project, it wasn't necessarily important for you to complete it perfectly; not at first, anyway. But as your creative side started to shine—when you started taking art and computer classes in high school—that proved to be a turning point: you cared more about the execution of things. Everything had to be JUST SO.

We quickly learned that change unsettled you. I had to let you know as soon as I could if there was going to be a change in our schedule because you found it so upsetting. You preferred order and stability and could become quite moody if things didn't go your way. But even though you tried us at times, there was always something special about you—a certain sparkle. Your charisma was magnetic. Out of our four children, you were the one our friends—and total strangers—would talk about. On those occasions when I was upset with you, I would repeat over and over to myself, "I know he is going to be something special."

You have definitely proven that statement to be true.

Today, I see a happy and fulfilled Connor who is in charge of himself, blazing his own trail. As your mother, I also see the love you have for your family and where you came from—and that warms my heart like your smile did twenty-two years ago.

Love, Mom

Dear Connor,

Connor Joel Franta, where do I begin? When I think of you as a child, many wonderful things come to mind. I would like to take all of the credit, given the fact I gave you billions of genes twenty-two years ago. Alas, I cannot. Your mother rightly deserves credit for the other half.

But I do see similarities between you and me: we share a passion for the water, we love anything to do with videos and photography, we both like to lead by example and we were both "chubby" as children (those genes you also got from me!). Growing up, you had a strong-willed personality, from the long and arduous time-outs that your mother has mentioned, to the early morning wake-hugs for school that brought grumpy replies of "Stop it, Dad!"

That will of yours ultimately translated into a fierce work ethic too, be it at sports or certain art projects. Such a tireless energy. Propelling your drive and determination, even motivated me!

I tried turning you into a wrestler. I had this image in my head that you'd be the next Dan Gable. He won gold in the Olympic Games in Munich in '72, and I envisioned you on that same podium. Wrestling was something I loved growing up, so I pushed you to like it, too. You never did.

Granted, you went along with my expectations for a while, trying to please me. We traveled to junior wrestling tournaments, and I felt proud that you placed fourth . . . out of four. You made the podium, and that was all that mattered! Even your sister, Nicola, tried to help you perfect your moves, teaching you how to do a single-leg take-down. That too ended in defeat with an injury. We have the video. It was painful to watch you struggle; even more painful for you to participate! I knew the Dan Gable dream was over when Nicola proved more into it than you were.

But looking back on that time, it was evident that you had a mind of your own. If you didn't want to do something, no one could make you. Stubbornness and a feisty nature were all part and parcel of that same strong will, as your younger brother Brandon could testify. You took out many of your frustrations on him!

Angry one minute, charismatic the next, we never really knew which Connor was going to show up, but your funny, dynamic personality made you popular with classmates. You were always going to blaze a trail of your own through life; of that, we were sure. There would be no stopping you.

It doesn't surprise me that you have built yourself into a techie, artistic, savvy, creative, brilliant YouTube sensation. You have always known your direction in life and carved out your own path, mile by mile. You will never know how proud I am of the man you have become. Not even words said face-to-face, or via text message, can do that pride justice.

Love, Dad

• • •

Is it safe to come out from behind the sofa now?

It's funny reading about how I behaved in the days before memories formed. So thanks for that input, Mom and Dad—wasn't so bad after all.

Now, this is normally the part of a memoir when the author spends *ages* retracing the steps of childhood, recounting endless episodes that are supposed to shed light on the adult he or she became. But my mind doesn't work that way. For me, childhood is a collection of snapshot memories and milestones, some of which might seem trivial to outsiders but left a lasting impression on me.

Here they are.

When I Was . . .

One: Dad taught me that life is all about being thrown into the deep end. My family was on our annual summer trip north to our cabin at White Earth Lake. With careful consideration, and after consulting a 1993 good-parenting guide, Dad decided to introduce me to the large body of water by throwing me in. Cool, Dad, real cool. He came with me obviously—and I didn't flail or freak out. And that was the moment he knew I was a water baby.

Four: I broke my brother's arm. It was a typical evening in the Franta household, until, that is, utter chaos unfolded. My younger brother, Brandon, was annoying the crap out of me (as much as any two-year-old could) and he pushed me to my breaking point. So I decided to push him off the chair he was standing on. He toppled, landed awkwardly, and broke his left arm. To this day, he hasn't let me live it down.

Five: Dad showed me and my siblings his prized roses that he'd nurtured and grown to perfection, impressing on us the importance of always keeping them watered. A few days later, he scolded me when he saw me standing there, peeing on them. I think I misunderstood. Look, when you gotta go, you gotta go. Plus, the plants looked veryyyy parched.

Six: I inadvertently became a shoplifter. I walked into a local convenience store and desperately wanted a piece of candy. When my parents said no, I defied them. We were just about back at our van when Dad noticed what I had done, hauled me back to the store—as any good parent trying to set an example would—and made me return the candy with a groveling apology. All I wanted was a Tootsie Roll. Geez.

Seven: I knew what I wanted to do when I was older: I wanted to have the same job as my dad and help people. I wanted to be a doctor. I recorded that in black and white, writing down my goal as part of a homework project.

Nine: I joined a swim team. My lovely mother signed me up. Being a chubby, relatively immobile child whose physical activities included eating and sleeping, let's just say I wasn't happy in the slightest. Begrudgingly, I started swimming lengths against the clock. I'm still convinced it was Mom's version of signing her son up for fat camp. Fortunately, it worked.

Ten: I accidentally killed a chipmunk. We were spending yet another summer at the family cabin, and my siblings and I were equipped with sick slingshots. Eager to practice my aim, I saw a tiny chipmunk crawling up a tree in the distance, so I took a shot—never thinking I'd get close—and hit him directly in temple. Suddenly I was Legolas from *Lord of the Rings* or Katniss from *The Hunger Games*. Cool? No. I felt horrible. I buried it on the beach and made every one of my family members attend the funeral.

When I grow up I want to be a doctor because I want to help people.

Twelve: I ran away from home. My brother and I got in a fight about something so minuscule and irrelevant that I can't remember the details, but things got really heated and I hopped on my bike and fled, vowing never to return. After pedaling two miles out of town, I got tired, a little hungry, and bored, so I went back. Life on my own was rough.

Fourteen: I landed my first job, at the local pool. I was excited to work a lengthy twenty hours a week, stacking baskets and manning the concession stand in hopes of working my way up to being a full-time lifeguard. I would live that dream the following year.

Fifteen: I received my first real kiss from a girl. It was in the hallway after school, and, afterward, I awkwardly stumbled away because my mom had pulled up in her minivan. The kiss felt weird, mainly because I didn't really enjoy it. *Hmm*, I thought to myself, *maybe I'll grow to like it.*

Sixteen: I had a brush with death. My sister, older brother, and I were returning home from some light Christmas shopping across the state border in Wisconsin. My sister was behind the wheel, and while on the bridge crossing the Mississippi River, we hit some black ice, spun out of control, and bounced off both sides of the concrete structure multiple times. The car was totaled, but we were lucky. My sister hates driving in the winter to this day.

Seventeen: Mom's faith in my athleticism paid off: I won my first state championship swimming title. It was a Friday night at the Wisconsin YMCA State Swim, and I was competing in the mile (1,650 yards). After racing neck and neck with seven other skilled competitors for just over seventeen minutes, I finished, looked up at the scoreboard, and saw the words: Connor Franta—First Place. I cried and ate a whole lot of spaghetti that night.

Levels of Friendship

O KAY, LET'S IMMERSE ourselves in a universally hated topic: school.

For me, grade school can be summed up to in two words: pleasant daze.

I never particularly enjoyed the mindless routine task that was the public education system. You'll never hear me say, "School days are the best days of your life," but then again, I didn't find them distasteful either. School was school—that necessary transition between being a kid and a grown-up; that bridge we all have to walk across—or, in my case, amble across.

I could write my own school report that summed me up as a student: "Connor is easily distracted, forever daydreaming, and, when not daydreaming, never stops talking. Yet learning inexplicably comes easily to him." Yes, I was one of those annoying kids who could pay attention 50 percent of the time, still absorb all the information, and walk away with A grades. Looking back, the best and most important part of school was developing my interests and, in turn, friendships. If you've seen any of my videos, you might rightfully assume that I never had trouble making friends growing up. I can be a little, um, in your face at times and pretty easy to talk to. I'm also just like incredibly likable *smiles and bats eyelashes.* Yes, I have friends and don't just sit on my computer all day.

I attended St. Peter's Catholic School from kindergarten to eighth grade. From the outside, this little redbrick building, perched on the corner of a street, looks like a church —probably because it's half church, half school—the community focal point of Hokah, Minnesota (population: 543). No, I'm not shitting you on that number, nor am I shitting you when I say that there were only sixty children at my school and FIVE in my class.

That's right: five—Glen, Vince, Andy, Jacob, and me, each with our own worn, wooden desk. Think *Little House on the Prairie,* and you'll

TIME CAPSULE

Fill in the information below.

Date _March 6th 2003_

Name _Connor Franta_

Age _14_

Address _____

Grade _8th_

My school name _St Peter's School_

My friends' names _Everyone_

My favorite teacher _There all ok._

My favorite subject _Math_

My favorite pet _My cat, Sam_

My favorite sport _Swimming_

My favorite TV show _Charmed_

My favorite games _Boulderdash_

My favorite Internet site _I don't have one_

My favorite instrument _None_

My favorite car _I don't know_

My favorite color _All_

My favorite hobbies or interests _Sports_

When I graduate from high school I want to: _Go to college and study something in the Medical department._

get the picture. It might also explain why attending St. Peter's was incredibly uneventful. I soon wanted more than the five boys in my grade to hang out with, and my restlessness clearly made itself known. "You were a little rascal growing up," Mrs. Lewis, my first-grade teacher, likes to remind me to this day. She's being nice by saying "rascal." I'm pretty sure half the teachers who taught me wanted to retire after we five stormed through their classroom—a mini-whirlwind causing much disruption. I'll say this, though: St. Peter's left quite the impression on me, enforcing kindness, intelligence, and good morals. "Do unto others what you would have them do unto you" was the golden rule painted on the wall of the stairwell. Read it. Learn it. LIVE IT! It also echoed everything my parents drilled into me. Being "the good boy" was the governing expectation. A fine message it was, too, even if I didn't immediately understand it. It took several years until I truly appreciated the strict letter of the moral law, as my classmate Jacob would testify.

One snowy winter's day on the playground, he got himself into trouble when he mouthed off to Mrs. Lewis, who was overseeing all sixty kids as they played tag or built an awesome fort in one of the snowbanks. For his boldness, she reserved him a sweet spot on the wall where he had to sit for a fifteen-minute time-out. "This isn't fair!" he kept saying, and I agreed with him. Most kids would just laugh, watch the friend mope away, and play with the other boys in the snow. Nope. Not me. Jacob was my best friend. I couldn't leave him standing there to either pass out from pure boredom or freeze to death like a kidsicle! In the spirit of loyalty, I walked toward the wall with the intent of standing next to him and honorably joining in on his punishment. But Mrs. Lewis was already wise to my thinking and intervened.

"Go play, Mr. Franta," she said. "This area is off-limits."

"Well, is there any way I can go over there with Jacob?"

"Nope," she said. "That area is only for kids who are in trouble."

"Okay," I said.

With that, the evil genius within me kicked in. I picked up a handful of snow, packed it together nicely to create a perfectly round snowball, and hurled it at the face of the nearest kid who was unfortunate enough to be walking by. SMACK! A direct hit.

I turned and looked directly at Mrs. Lewis. "Oops, guess I'm in trouble too." Young Connor was dastardly, I'm telling you.

Sure enough, an angry Mrs. Lewis sent me into the trouble zone and I ended up sitting against the same wall with Jacob. That act solidified a friendship that continues to this day. Now, I'm not saying you have to hit a poor, random child in the face with a snowball to have good friendships—or am I? No. No, I'm not.

I don't think . . .

No, the point of this story is that there are only a select few friends, past or present, that I would go to such lengths to stand by. That's what school really taught me: the enduring nature of friendship. How special it is to grow up and share a history with someone. As I've gotten older, friendships rooted in childhood feel even richer and more irreplaceable.

Friendship. Now there's an interesting topic. I've always appeared to have a lot of friends, but appearances can be deceiving. Sure, I know a lot of people and am comfortable saying "hi" to them in the street, shooting them a text saying we should grab a coffee, or going on Facebook to wish them a happy birthday, but where does that rank them in terms of friendship?

For me, there are distinct levels of friendship:

BEST FRIEND: An extremely close individual you can do anything with, talk about everything with, confide in, and be comfortable with sitting in silence on car journeys; those people you consider to be part of your family

GOOD FRIEND: A person you are comfortable hanging out with one-on-one for an extended period of time and see semiregularly; someone who shares experiences with you but not your deepest troubles and secrets

FRIEND: Someone you hang out with in a group setting occasionally

ACQUAINTANCE: Someone you know on a first-name basis and say "hi" to but that's pretty much the extent of it

STRANGERS: The rest of the world (and all your potential best friends in the future)

I would rather have 1
amazing best friend than
100 decent regular friends.
It's not about quantity,
it's about quality.

Recently, and more than ever before, I realized that I have three best friends, a dozen good friends, a whole bunch of friends, an even bigger bunch of acquaintances, and billions of strangers in my own life.

Ranking where people stand in your life and who they are to you helps you determine who you value the most and therefore where best to spend your time. Truth be told, I don't have too many people who are close to me. That was kind of scary to realize at first, but I've also found a strange sense of comfort in it. You want to know why? Well, I'm going to tell you.

Friends are not a number. You can't collect connections. You can't just go out one day and be like, "Hey, I need some friends!" *goes shopping, scours social media*

Don't count the number of "friends" you have on Facebook or the followers you have on Twitter, Tumblr, or Instagram. True friendship is counted in memories, experiences, and troubles shared; it's a bond built up over time in person, not a virtual tally on the Internet. It finds you; you don't find it. A relationship forms, you discover common interests, and you realize this bond is the closest thing to romance that is possible. Yes, that's it: true friendship is a relationship without sex or attraction. It doesn't judge, gossip, flake, and get envious. It stands by you through thick and thin. It supports you at your lowest ebb and celebrates with you at your highest point. It allows you to be yourself, good and bad. And it's a two-way street: you give and take equally.

As you get older, sometimes your goals will take you away from your closest friends. Literally. Two of my best friends now live in different countries than I do. Now, you're probably thinking, *Connor, it must take some real work to keep up those relationships.* Wrong. The best part about best friends is that you can maintain a relationship at any distance. In this day and age, we have Skype, FaceTime, text messages, audio messages, photo messages, and every social media site you can think of. With my friends, I send little photo updates almost daily and do a video call every week. It's really not that difficult. We talk about anything and everything. I can confide my deepest, darkest secrets with my best friends and fear no judgment. It's actually the best. And when we have the luxury of being in the same location, we pick things up like we were never separated. It really doesn't matter where we go or what we do; it's honestly just so nice to be in each other's presence that the rest doesn't matter.

Whether it's the friends who have walked with you or the friends who await you in the future, the value of true friendship is golden. Know this too: Some people won't like you, and you won't like everyone. That's okay. None of that matters. What matters is meeting like-minded people who get you, accept you, and will do anything for you. Even if that means pegging some poor kid in the face with a snowball and sitting against a playground wall on a cold, snowy day.

Moon Gazing

I remember cool autumn nights when a couple of friends and I would walk a few blocks from my house to a park: playground dead ahead, baseball field to the right, or soccer field to the left. We'd always head left to the middle of the field where it seemed darker and quieter, and we would lie down, hands tucked under our heads, looking up at the sky, as clear as can be.

This was one of my favorite things to do as a teenager. It still is.

Lying there, the silence seemed to pierce my every pore, thought, and sense. On chilly nights in Minnesota, you can see every star and twinkle in the deep void above. Not only is it visually stunning, it always shifts my perspective, reminding me how small we are on earth—tiny specks in a tiny city on a tiny globe suspended in a vast universe. We really are minuscule in the grand scheme of things.

I know this experience sounds very much like *The Fault in Our Stars;* if you've read that book or seen that movie, you can probably imagine the scene. In this case, I'm Shailene Woodley. But all cheese factor aside, it's a great way to be with friends and reflect and open up. When I'm with my friends, we usually talk about anything and everything for an hour or so. Nothing else matters; it's almost a worry-free zone. All feelings, opinions, thoughts, and emotions are fair game. No judgment. I love a long evening at the park. It refreshes my soul and enhances my perspective.

Missing Out

HATE MISSING OUT—always have and probably always will. I remember especially feeling this way when I was younger, as this story illustrates.

I'm eight, it's a weekend, and the whole family is at home, not doing very much. My dad, being the good father he is, decides to treat me to a one-on-one father-son outing. I'm playing with toys in my bedroom when he walks in smiling, eager to begin the fun plans he has in store. "Con! How about you and I drive down to the lake, fish for a bit, then get some ice cream! How's that sound?"

Sounds good, I think. But there's a *but*. Somewhat skeptical, I say, "Um, well, what is everyone else going to do while we're gone?" Dad laughs. "I don't know! But hey, they definitely won't have as much fun as us." That was the reassurance I was seeking. "Good," I reply. "No fun. I don't want them to do anything while we're gone. Just sit and not move." Dad probably thought I was being unintentionally cute, but I meant it. I didn't want anyone to have fun until we were back, because I wouldn't be there to share it with them. Oh, what a little shit I was.

I rarely missed out on much . . . and yet it still bothered me.

Funny thing is, I'm still the same today (not the little shit part; more the not-wanting-people-to-have-fun-when-I'm-not-there part). The thought of friends or family enjoying themselves in my absence gives me the heebie-jeebies. (Side note: Does any breathing human even use that phrase anymore—*heebie-jeebies*? I know I normally don't. Who am I? Who are you?? How did I get here??? GO AWAY!)

But anyway, I have often wondered what this particular trait was all about and I recently figured it out, thanks to a friend. "Oh, you have FOMO," he said, as though it were an everyday, medically diagnosed condition.

"I have what?!" I responded, thinking it was some deadly disease.

"FOMO. Fear Of Missing Out."

He wasn't joking. It's in Urban Dictionary. It's legit. Look it up.

Where YOLO (You Only Live Once) is about having the time of your life, FOMO is its polar opposite—and resides within me. I know I'm not alone in this. We've all tasted it, especially on those weekend nights when you've chosen to stay in and then see your friends post on social media about their fun evening out, and you squirm with jealousy.

Social media makes this condition ten times worse. Everyone is constantly posting little updates in real time for everyone else to see, so you know what you're missing at every waking moment. I know exactly when and where family, friends, and acquaintances are enjoying a refreshing juice or artery-clogging burger. It's terrible. No place online is safe. You can't go on the Internet. You're forced to do things like . . . like . . . like read a *book*. EW.

I recognized this social curse as soon as my friend diagnosed it.

Suddenly there was a label to some unknown feeling I had normalized and become accustomed to. *Yeah, that makes sense*, I thought. After some deep reflection this light-bulb moment induced, I soon pinpointed where this feeling comes from in me: middle child syndrome. (There's always someone or something else to blame, right?)

Take it from a middle child; being a middle child sucks. You have neither the responsibility that comes with being the oldest nor the luxury that comes with being the baby. You have N O T H I N G. No label. No identity. Not to mention my fellow middle child, Nicola, was the only girl in the family. See! Nothing! You're the in-between child, squeezed into the order of things. You're the Idaho to New York and Los Angeles. You're the regular-sized cup in between the large and small. (I actually like a good medium-sized drink, to be quite honest, but you get the point.)

Ugh, what a rough life we middle children live. Feel bad for us, okay? OKAY!!?! Okay.

My mom has since confirmed that my overeager go-to response—when I was going anywhere or had anything planned for me—was, "What's everyone else going to do?"

"We noticed a change in your temperament following the birth of your brother Brandon, and that coincided with our move to La Crescent and you turning two years old," she recently told me. "Dad and I would try to spend some one-on-one time with you, but you were always afraid of missing out on something at home. No one was allowed to have fun if you weren't there!"

My poor parents. What did I put them through?!

But I genuinely worried about it. I worried about being left out

to such a degree that even when I wasn't being left out, I still worried about missing out.

Of course, the truth is that my position in the family wasn't as bad as I have depicted. I just made it out to be bad (because I'm not-so-secretly dramatic). That's not to say that the extent of my fear wasn't true. There have been instances when I've spent more time worrying that I'm missing out on something than actually enjoying what's right in front of me. And there, my friends, is the lesson to be learned.

Life should be more about living in the moment than fearing what's happening outside it. It's about honoring what you want to do at any given time, regardless of what everyone else is doing. There's no use worrying about things that are out of your control.

As I get older, I'd like to think I have my FOMO under control, but by no means is it gone. I still can't help but cringe a little when I see my friends out doing something fun while I'm stuck at home all alone. But I immediately tell myself, "Hey. If you don't want to be alone, don't be alone, stupid. Text one of your friends and go do something." It's as simple as that. If someone responds, I'm very happy to live in that moment with that person. If no one does, I enjoy the alone time and appreciate the silence. I've learned it's completely all right to do that, too—be alone, that is. It gives me a good excuse to catch up on my Netflix addiction. Everyone wins.

All in all, I'm learning to tame the shady jealousy demon that's been with me since childhood. There have been numerous occasions when, consumed with inexplicable fear, I have hated being where I was because I knew—or believed—there was somewhere better to be. That middle child reared his head and started looking around, getting fidgety. In moments like this, I'm left with two options:

1. Make that unfortunate situation better by allowing myself to have a good time.
2. Make an effort to be where I want to be and don't waste my time elsewhere.

These days, I won't miss out if there's nowhere else I would rather be. Plain and simple. We cannot do everything; we cannot be everywhere. If you want to have a good time, make it a good time! If you want to sit and sulk about how bored and uneventful things are, cool! Enjoy that. It sounds amazing—in a weird, dark, antisocial kind of way. But I've been there. I've worried needlessly. The doubt, the distaste, the what-is-happening-elsewhere was all in my head. A complete waste of energy. So that's it. I'm saying NO MORE to FOMO. I suggest you do the same.

I'm looking forward to graduating this year. I think it will be fun going to high school. I'm looking forward to all the fieldtrips this year; like skiing and going to Valley Fair. I'm not looking forward to the huge history tests.

From,
Connor

High school will be fun for you, and so will this year!!

Mrs. Fishel

High School Is Weird

AFTER LIVING UP my education at St. Peter's for nine years, it was time to get the heck out of there and move on to bigger (hardly) and better (hardly) things: high school. *dramatically zooms in, screams; horror music plays in the background* I left my Catholic school with a good head on my shoulders and a decent reputation, but this was definitely a dramatic shift, even though I was still in La Crescent. I went from a world of sixty students to one with around five hundred, from a humble brick shack to an institution with halls specific to each grade and dozens of teachers. The scale of everything was dizzying, but at least it was only two miles from my house. The convenience was, well, convenient.

Walking in through the gates on my first day, I was surprised how I took all this in my stride. Not at all scared. In fact, I was excited for the change because I believed what the teachers said: my whole future lay ahead of me.

Nicola, a junior that year, drove me to school on my first day, and that probably helped calm the nerves too. On the way there, I did wonder about certain things. *Will it be the same as the movies, with bullies, scary seniors, horrible lunches, and centuries of homework?* Doubtful. *Will I make friends easily?* Probably. *Are these going to be the best years of my life?* I freaking hope not! But such questions faded into insignificance when measured against the bigger issues on my mind: forgetting my locker combo, not being able to find my classes, and sitting alone at lunch. Rough life, right? But isn't that what we all do in high school? Overthink things and worry about what's out of our control?

We all need to calm down!

In that first year of school, I was emerging from that superawkward phase where every feeling is magnified and disproportionate.

I didn't know how to be social outside of my friendships, and I can't say that I was the most gregarious student.

I remember giving my first speech during a class presentation freshman year and, boy, did I sweat bullets. I've always had a fear of public speaking. I think most people do. It's hard to be confident standing up in front a room full of people, with them staring you down and scrutinizing the delivery of every one of your words. I'm beginning to shake just at the thought of it. I. HATE IT. There's something about being the center of attention in that specific way just gets my blood moving and my heart racing.

Even today, I get nervous speaking in front of big crowds. It's not like a YouTube video, which I can film, edit, and post from the security and comfort of my apartment. Public speaking means the people are real and right in front of you. I've gotten better at public speaking with age, but by no means am I comfortable with it. But, anyways back to the story.

I got up in front of the class to do my speech, gave one huge gulp, opened my mouth, and began. "Hello everyasdfghjkl"—and at that moment, my voice stumbled and cracked louder than it ever had before. Everyone giggled, and my face turned redder than a tomato. Somehow I soldiered on, got a B-, and moved on with my life. What's funny about looking back on that excruciating moment is that speaking is now my job. It could have completely stifled my confidence, but I had to own it so I could get over it. To this day, my voice STILL cracks, but now I roll with the punches, make a few self-deprecating jokes, and continue. Some things never really change. You can only control your perspective. If you do, the big things that haunted you at school seem so pointless.

Aside from pubescent self-consciousness, I was a good, well-behaved teenager. It was rare that I received anything lower than an A or was anything short of an innocent angel. But high school made me realize what a sheltered life I had lived until then. I saw kids rebel. I heard them swear. And I had no idea what the hell this "weed" thing was that everyone mentioned in passing. Me, the goody-two-shoes, walked around thinking, *Is this what real life is like?* I'd never had a real relationship, hardly ever swore, never tried a drop of alcohol, and certainly hadn't experimented with drugs. But of course, purity doesn't last forever, and I soon became engulfed in this new world of teenage angst and rebellion. Okay. I'm making it sound like I became a drug addict and had lots of sex, but hold up! That wasn't the case. I just became exposed to the world, like the blinders had been removed. In typical good-kid fashion, I never really experienced the "bad" things I was around, but my awareness of them increased.

Maybe all this exposure had an indirect impact of me because in my junior year, things began to change and the inner rebel began to emerge. I didn't care if my homework wasn't done to absolute perfection. I stayed out late with friends, even on school nights. Hey, I even went to a few parties! I most definitely came out of my shell. And I don't regret it, though I did some things that were out of character for me—the consequences of trying to care less. I failed several tests, got pulled over a few times for speeding, and stayed out late instead of taking care of my responsibilities. My parents eventually had to have a little chat with me about it, which forced me to realize that I wasn't being me. Yeah, my "bad boy" phase was by no means bad compared to some of the other kids around me—you wouldn't believe some of the horror stories I heard and witnessed—but it still didn't make it okay. I started to see myself in a bad light, and I knew I had to reevaluate my priorities. So that's what I did.

I went back to the old me.

This is what happens in high school. We're exposed to what's not familiar while trying to work out who we are. We explore, make bad decisions, and learn from them. I may have not made any life-changing mistakes, but I witnessed many friends meet the consequences of some ill-considered choices. So I watched and learned instead of actually committing the crimes myself. Not so bad, if you ask me. High school, like any other new environment, can feel weird at first, but that's also the challenge of our teen years: being able to adapt. I noticed how everyone seemed to gravitate toward the cliquey friend groups they had in middle school, which sucked because I hadn't gone to the same school as everyone else. But I had some friends from sports, so I figured that if I sidled up and stood silently by them, they would introduce me to their friends, and I would collect friends by association.

My plan worked.

It wasn't the worst thing in the world to be the new kid. At one of the first football games, just a couple of weeks in, one girl said to me, "Everyone is obsessed with you, Connor!" "Wait. What??" I said, shocked. "Why?!?" "I don't know! They all think you're cute and good at sports and stuff!"

What shallow standards for liking someone, I thought. *But I'll take it!*

Little did they know that I didn't feel cool at all. But, hey, I was okay with living the lie as long as my social status benefited. And that's totally what I did in high school. Faked it 'til I made it. And improvised. I did a lot of improvising. That's the downside of growing up. There's a lot of pretending involved. We frequently act like someone other than who we really are because we don't know or aren't comfortable with our true selves. "Just be yourself," parents and grandparents often say, but that's easier said than done. It seems we must grow up before we can even begin to think about flourishing. It's taken me years to realize and embrace this.

I loved what that girl said at the football game because I so desperately wanted to be seen as a cool kid, regardless of how cliché that sounds. I cared far too much about what I wore and how I spoke; hell, I even began to worry about the words that would come out of my mouth. Did they sound cool enough?

The idea of not being accepted was scary. *Look cool and be cool*, I always thought. After a couple of trips to the rundown mall across the river, going in and out of fitting rooms—there were only three stores to choose from, so my new style was very limited. Mom, aka my personal stylist and fashion guru, judged me head to toe, and she and I both liked what we saw.

I was happy with my new look: more fitted jeans, nonathletic shoes, and a cool graphic tee. Yes, they were back in then. (Don't give me that look.) I felt ready to brave the judgment zone that is high school. My pretend-cool was so thick that it felt like a suit of armor—an armor of confidence. I told myself that if the high stan-

dards were not met, I'd suck up the dreaded disapproving glances and backhanded compliments. As it was, I clocked more approving glances and noted a few admiring whispers as well. At least, I think they were admiring. Maybe everyone thought I was ugly and trying too hard. Whatever, I don't want to know the truth now.

Regardless, all that pressure you feel when you're growing up—especially self-imposed pressure—is not fun. It's no walk in the park to feel as if all eyes are on you, even when 99 percent of the time they're actually not. Each gender has it bad. Boys have to live up to these big, athletic, manly standards, while girls feel they need to be sweet, best-dressed, flawless-faced robots. It is here, in high school, that the seeds are first laid fostering the myth of what is masculine and what is feminine—how men and women should be. The truth is that no one HAS to be anything. You leave school, look back, and realize how insignificant all that thinking and worrying was.

Girls can be athletic. Guys can have feelings. Girls can be smart. Guys can be creative. And vice versa. Gender is specific only to your reproductive organs (and sometimes not even to those), not your interests, likes, dislikes, goals, and ambitions. Guys need feminine energy as much as girls need masculine energy to get by in the world. These are the things they don't write on the chalkboard with the mathematical proofs.

I felt this pressure when I was a teenager. It just wasn't cool to be effeminate in any way at my school. Whether that meant dressing well, enjoying art, or being dramatic, I felt I had to be constantly aware of how I presented myself out of fear that I would be seen as too feminine. In my experience, the social structure that many people unintentionally follow is too black-and-white for boys or girls to cross the line of perceived gender norms. It was exhausting to have

to pretend to be macho, enjoy football, and hate anything creative. That just wasn't me.

When I first thought that I liked art—that art is fun—I was hesitant to act on that because I didn't want to come across as girly or feminine for being creative. I suppressed my artsy side and held myself back from pursuing the things I wanted to do: plays, art classes, and clubs. Those things were scary to participate in because of my fear of being looked down on. It took me years to slowly get over all that and just do it. What a shame.

Now, four years out of high school, I'm in an environment where people appreciate personality over appearance, and that makes me happy. In a broader cultural sense, some of the shallow standards are being remade as "alternative" people claim more of the spotlight, but there is still work to be done. Only once we can all accept that what matters is on the inside, not the outside, then our society will truly progress.

LCHS homecoming royalty crowned

Connor Franta and Libby Kathan were named 2010 La Crescent High School homecoming royalty Monday. Homecoming concludes with Friday's football game.

RYAN HENRY/HOUSTON COUNTY NEWS

An Anxious Boy and His Plastic Crown

I'M SITTING ON A STAGE in my high school auditorium, and the entire student body is staring at me, weighing my royal prospects. Thank the Lord none of my family is present—that would only add to the nerves. Next to me, in this indoor theater of sorts, five other juniors are filled with equal trepidation, if not quite as much dread. (Some are in school plays; others are star athletes and love being on stage.)

We've all been nominated for homecoming king, and today is "crowning day."

Autumn is coming to an end, so the air has a slight chill that doesn't help my already clammy appearance. With all seats in the theater filled, I hate that everyone is gaping at me. I don't want to be here. I don't want to win this award and be "crowned" in front of five hundred people. That would be torture. Cruelty. Well, okay, it's not that bad, but you get the idea of how mortifying this whole experience feels for me.

For the past two weeks, my name has been plastered around school. I see people check the box next to my name—the mark that says they prefer me to anyone else on the sheet. I've had people issuing hearty congratulations on the nomination. "Hope you win!" they yell, getting all giddy. Neat. Win what? A plastic crown? Cool.

If you look at any of my online work, you might assume I'm a huge extrovert. I wouldn't say you're 100 percent wrong—more like 62 percent, to be exact. I just don't like a certain kind of attention. Yeah, sure, I enjoy hanging out in social situations and love talking and interacting with other humans, but that's about me expressing myself, about being in a room full of people feeding off each other's positive energy.

Being evaluated while I sit on a stage is not about that.

I'm telling myself that if I win, I'm going to pull a Cady Heron *Mean Girls* act. (It's going to happen.) She can't believe it when she's nominated for Spring Fling queen. She knows the sense of humiliation that comes with the applause. (Actually she kind of enjoys it, but I still want to break my crown and throw it at the audience if I win. It's kind of a dream of mine. I love that movie.)

While waiting on stage, I'm hoping one of my five peers will be anointed. We sit there and a teacher tells us that one of the boxes in front of us—the ones at each of our feet—contains the crown. A sort of *Deal or No Deal* format. "If you have the crown in your box, you're homecoming king!" *dramatic music begins to play* Hesitantly, I begin to open the carefully taped box. I break the seal. I look to my left, hoping to see someone else pulling out a crown to big cheers.

I dig through the tissue paper inside and—oh God, no—there it is: the hideous plastic crown that probably cost five dollars at Walmart. I'm cringing at the thought.

My stomach sinks as I keep my head down, trying to pretend that I haven't seen anything. But the guy to my immediate right notices and starts pointing, and the whole place erupts in cheers. I have no choice but to stand and claim my title, let them put the crown on my head as my cheeks blush bright red, and walk to the center of the stage. I'm joined by my queen, appearing from my left, and everyone applauds.

I'm dying behind the smiles and can't even think straight enough to follow my *Mean Girls* plan. *sigh*

Okay, don't get me wrong, I'm incredibly flattered that people apparently liked me in high school. I guess that's cool, but I don't like the quality of that kind of attention or how it makes me feel; that's what it all comes down to. I don't want all eyes on me in the center of the ring just like a circus. It makes me sweat. But that's what this crowning ceremony brought: a whole load of attention. I wasn't the extrovert that kingly role demanded.

Here's what I think people sometimes have trouble understanding about people like me. Yes, I'm a vlogger, but I do it from the privacy of my own home, confined by walls. While I don't squirm under attention as much as I did back then, I'm also very okay with not having all eyes on me. This is something that anyone close to me would tell you: I'm somewhat shy, not a show-off. I'm a flower that doesn't require a lot of sunlight. Make sense?

Looking back on that day, I think it's a really cool story to tell people. I'm fortunate to have been part of that ceremony, as much as

I didn't enjoy it at the time. It's not something I regret; surprisingly, I learned a lot about who I am. That's what high school is all about: finding yourself, figuring out what makes you tick. I realized I like to blend in and go relatively unnoticed. Oh, the irony. Oh, the joys of being a complicated human.

But there you have it—that's the story of the day I became a reluctant king—and discovered that not all attention is created equal.

The Voice Within

A S A KID, I WAS never afraid to have a different opinion on
things. Dad says he saw that in the wrestler I didn't become. I see
it more in the day when I purchased my first laptop in ninth grade,
which might seem like a mundane thing but was a pretty formative
experience in my journey toward creative expression. It wasn't just
any laptop, though. It was a MacBook. BUM-BUM-BUMMMM!
The screams of opinionated PC-users echo loudly in the distance

Before I made this big purchase, I of course had to ask my dad
if it was okay to buy a computer that he hadn't heard of—and neither had anyone else in the family and immediate friend group. But I
thought Apple products were cool. I'd spent hours researching and,
frankly, fantasizing about this leap into the future. It was like technological porn to me. Its sleek design, unique operating system, built-in
creative programs, and undeniable beauty made the inner geek in me
melt into a puddle. I had saved up the money, but it was still a thousand dollars, which probably explained why I was so nervous about
broaching the subject.

"Daaad?" I said, walking into my parents' bedroom while they were still sleeping. I thought that if I caught him half-awake, he'd say, "Yes, go ahead."

"Huh, what??" he groaned, head not moving on the pillow.

"I want to ask your opinion about something."

"Okay," he said in his morning voice. "What's up?"

"Wellll, I really want to buy the new MacBook that just came out because it's really cool and pretty and amazing and it's a thousand dollars and I have the money and . . . and . . . um, yeah."

Unfortunately, that didn't come out as confidently as I wanted—and he sat up.

"Oh, Con, that's a lot of money. Wouldn't you rather get a five-hundred-dollar PC instead? It's half the price, and they work great!"

Parents don't understand cool. Never have. Never will.

So it was time to impart my well-researched knowledge. Parents like facts, not emotions—facts delivered with certainty. Know this before stating your impassioned case. Do your homework. If your parents respond with emotion to your facts and due diligence, they lose. Remember that, even if *you* lose.

"Dad, I've looked into this, and MacBooks last way longer and are made for more creative people and . . ." I bombarded him with the genius of this gadgetry, from its tools to its battery life to its cost-effectiveness. "It'll be more than worth the money. It's like an investment!" I added.

Dad had no comeback except, "Well, I can't stop you from spending your own money, but I don't think it's a wise decision, Connor." Long story short, I ignored his caution and bought that gorgeous piece of aluminum ten minutes later.

Going into that conversation, it didn't really matter what my dad said. I knew what I wanted, knew what I liked, and nothing was going to change that. The point of this story is not that I got my own way, or that I've never been happier with a decision, or that this very laptop was the one on which I taught myself how to edit graphics and videos in iMovie and images in Photoshop—truly where my passion began and potentially the only reason I am doing what I'm doing today. No, all that is the result of the point I'm making: know what you want and follow your gut.

It's hard to truly know what you want and who you are. It's even harder to attune yourself to that inner voice that tells you what your heart is saying. You know it when something feels off, when you bristle, when you hear one big, fat screaming "NO!" in your head.

Whatever the personal decision—in conversation, friendship, dating, career—pay attention to what your gut says, and not necessarily what you're told and what you think you should think (because then you'll overthink it). Whether it's buying my first MacBook, or all the other decisions I made that you'll learn about in this book, I always stick with my gut decision. I never let the opinions of others fog my own judgment. It has guided me to where I am today and shaped how I approach every difficult decision and situation.

In a world conditioned to follow the herd mentality, a lot of people find it hard to stay true to themselves and accept the things particular to them. It's easy to give in to peer pressure and simply settle with what everyone else is doing, but never forget that each of us is different. You are your own individual, with your own particular set of dreams, desires, and aspirations. Everyone has preferences unique to him or her. So know what you like, know what makes you happy, stick to your guns, and state it with confidence.

You'll walk taller, and as long as you follow your gut, you won't stray far in life.

Vintage

I have vintage tastes. I love anything vintage, from Polaroid cameras to record players. There's something about their simplicity that I find appealing. There are no viewfinders, digital zoom, or image enhancements of any kind. It's just raw and real.

With an old camera, the focus is on the process of taking a photo because you can't see what you've captured until it's been developed. There's no going back. It is what is it. The preparation for the shot matters most. If you mess up, you won't know until it's too late. And let's be real, is there any better sound than a Polaroid snap or the anticipation of watching your photo emerge into reality? Probably. But it really tickles my fancy.

With a record player, you hear music in its most authentic form (aside from live performances, of course.) Everything feels vulnerable; the lack of bass, the slight crackle on vinyl, and the shining voice fuse together to create an atmosphere that makes me feel completely connected to the artist. I can't get enough of it.

Both of these vintage products transport me to the analog age, a time my parents remember well—and I remember from when I was a kid. Not everything has to be digital or downloaded. There is a traditional, minimalist beauty to the Polaroid and record player and being immersed in the true vintage experience each provides.

Worth It

HAD A LOVE-HATE relationship with my first job as a lifeguard. At fourteen (is that even legal??), I was ecstatic when I was hired to work at the local outdoor pool—a small, concrete hole in the ground known as La Crescent City Pool. And, boy, was it AWESOME! I couldn't wait to be independent and make my own money.

That philosophy—to be free and stand on my own two feet— stuck with me for the first three or four years there, and it was rewarding work, teaching kids how to swim and improve their abilities on the swim team. But after a while, the—how do I say this—repetitive nature of the job started to slowly suck away my happiness, bit by bit. It was essentially a 9-to-5 job, except my "office" was an elevated lifeguard chair where I sat for hours on end, listening to repetitive country music, or counting the beads of sweat dripping down my arm in the very hot and humid midwestern weather. Sitting out in the hot summer sun, watching kids yell at each other while nearly drowning, can be draining—and totally not worth the minimum wage. Plus, I was working forty- to fifty-hour weeks all summer long while saving up for whatever the future held for me while my friends were off having fun. That didn't make it any better.

I started hating it all, from the sweat stains on my everywhere to the screaming kids who never listened. Sometimes, I had to be up for work at 5:00 a.m. Sometimes I had to clean toilets or, worse, scoop the feces of children out of the shallow end of the pool in front of dozens of people, and then have them be mad at me for closing down the pool for an hour while it was cleaned. As if it were my fault the pool had been mistaken for a toilet. MY BAD.

It was grueling work, but I shouldn't complain, because although it was difficult at times, all the stress was worth it on one particularly rewarding day.

It was a chilly summer evening in June 2008—one of those evenings when the sun hasn't shined in days and there is a distinct moistness to, well, everything. Only a few kids remained in the pool, and it was my turn to oversee them.

One kid in particular caught my attention—a bored-looking boy sitting in the shallow end, doing nothing but seemingly watch his life go by.

Why are you here? I thought, *Go hoooooome.*

I almost felt like verbalizing this thought on one of my walks around the pool, but then he spoke: "Today I want to pass my swimming test!"

Okay, good. At least now you're doing SOMETHING.

I led this sweet-faced boy over to the deep end, with the aim of watching him swim from one end of the pool to the other. I had watched many kids do this, day in and day out, so I didn't even think twice about it as he climbed down the short ladder into the shiver-inducing water.

Standing there, I watched him slowly tackle the short distance ahead of him. He wasn't the most fluent of swimmers; he had quite a heavy technique but was slowly making progress. But then, with about ten feet to go, the reason for his quiet contemplation in the shallow end started to dawn on me: he doubted if he was capable. He wasn't the strongest of swimmers.

He started to slow up, then came to a total halt and began to bob like an apple. Dammit.

Oh no, I thought, is this going to happen? TODAY, of all days?! Am I actually going to have to save a living, breathing person from drowning?! It was cold, I had a sweatshirt on, and all I had been focused on was going home. And that was when I saw his head turn to look at me, like a person does when he's adrift.

"H-h-help," he kind of whispered, panic evident in his voice.

Well, here we go, I thought.

I blew my whistle, sending a piercing screech through the air, kicked off my sandals, and dove in with my red lifeguard tube. He was struggling, arms flailing as he battled to keep his chin above water, but I soon had him out. The poor kid was a little shaken up but otherwise okay. His mom was mighty relieved too when I took him, all bundled up, to the pool house and told her what had happened. She was slightly angry that I "took too long to jump in," but I get it. It's her kid. Every second seems like an eternity if someone you love is in trouble.

That night, I too blew a sigh of relief. And at that moment, everything sank in: I had just saved a life. Without me, that kid would have probably DIED. That was a sobering thought, putting into context all those 5:00 a.m. starts, poop-scooping incidents, and long hours. It all made sense at that point.

Sometimes we lose sight of why we're doing what we're doing. We get sick of certain aspects of our lives and forget the end goal. But everything has a purpose. There is a reason behind every struggle, and I finally understood mine. Minimum wage aside, I signed up to be a lifeguard to help kids. I have a driving passion for anything water related and wanted to share that with fresh minds. And when the time came that one of those minds really needed my help, I was there for him.

I slept very well that night and finished out my following summers of work at the pool with a new perspective. Sometimes that's all it takes to find meaning in what you're doing.

My Arm

If you go through my Instagram, you'll notice a recurring theme: photos of my arm, extended. "Why do you do that?" people always ask, usually in a slightly irritated tone. "I don't get it. Stop doing that. It's so Tumblr," they say.

My answer? I like placing myself in my photography. It's difficult to do when you're also taking the photo, so I suppose just an arm will do. A forearm in the frame is a bit like a toe in the water. Whenever I find myself somewhere beautiful and interesting, I just take a photo of my hand pointing at the scene I wish to remember. So, now you know.

Connor

Creativity

HANDS UP IF YOU'RE CREATIVE. (I'm now visualizing a room filled with hands reaching to the ceiling.)

Now keep your arm raised if you feel that you're able to freely pursue that creativity.

(My mind's eye sees a few arms lower in disappointment.)

Okay. For those of you still reaching skyward, how many feel brave enough to show your creative side and put it out there without first nervously running it by friends or family?

I suspect most of you are sitting on your hands, thinking, *Nope. I'm out. Not me.*

I would have been one of those kids sitting on my hands a few years ago. I love to create. I love creating concepts and content, starting from nothing. Heck, I love to create my breakfast in the morning (a work of art in itself!). But during my school years, I felt discouraged. It's not cool to be artsy by general teenage boy standards, and that intimidated me, so I pushed my creativity away.

I wanted to be to be in, not out.

By being creative, you have to be okay with putting your work out there for public scrutiny. Whether you're painting, acting in a school play, or screening a short film you created in film class, it's scary to stand out and be vulnerable. What if you're criticized for doing what you're doing? That's even more terrifying.

Now, before I go any further, I know not everyone is interested in the arts, and that's totally okay. Whether your passion leads you to be a janitor, nurse, fitness instructor, artist, or athlete later in life, my message is broad: wholeheartedly pursue your passions. Do the things you love and love the things you do.

From recent conversations I've had on this topic, having your creativity stifled at a young age appears to be the sad truth for a lot of people. Sure, I was encouraged to practice the arts at a young age, but as I grew older, I felt a distinct pressure to follow the path of a more practical career. It seems some of our imaginative peers suppress their artistic instincts out of fear of being judged, alienated, or just plain not good enough. In other cases, a parent, teacher, or friend has been dismissive about creative ambitions. Don't let that suffocate your vision. More often than not, people won't share your vision or hunger, but that's all right. Ambitions are individual. Art is subjective. Creativity often leads to the solo pursuit of a dream until you find like-minded people who get it. Who get *you*.

I'm talking here to every budding writer, poet, singer/songwriter, musician, actor, entertainer, dancer, sculptor, director, photographer, circus act, trapeze artist, pole dancer, whatever! We live in a world where the importance of stability is drilled into us from an early age. If it's not explicitly stated, then it is seen in the way most of our parents, other elders, or authority figures live their lives: cautiously, pragmatically, and sensibly.

There is nothing certain about even contemplating a career rooted in your creative dream, whatever that may be. The potential risk of failure screams its warning from far away, which is why those with experience feel it is necessary to tell us to find "proper jobs"—the kind that pay well and guarantee long-term security. "Be a lawyer, a doctor, or a teacher," they say. But there is one thing they can't hear: the silent beat of creativity within you—that calling beckoning you to trust your gut, follow your heart, and do what your soul demands. You can never articulate to others what you feel in your bones because you rarely understand it yourself. Do you know how many times I get a bomb-ass idea but can't explain it to anyone? All. The. Time. They can't see it, but I can—and that's all that matters. They will see it when I bring my idea to life.

If you are one of those people—if you hear that calling—that is the ONLY thing you should listen to, be it a one-time project you yearn to do or a career you know you must pursue. Never deny yourself the opportunity for self-expression, in any form.

Don't underestimate the power of self-belief.

Don't be limited by the expectations of others.

Don't care what anybody else thinks.

"But what's the point of trying? I'm just going to fail," someone once said to me. And my response was simple: "So what? Who cares? If you fail, you fail. Big deal." Success involves failing first. Ask any successful person. Ask any experienced person, really. It's all part of the creative process, so sit back and allow the artist within you to sprout, blossom, and flourish. You must accept that your first, second, and third attempt at something might suck. It's a necessary step in improving your skill. Failure is your teacher, not your judge.

Like any other good thing, it takes time, and you'll just have to wait it out. All you have to know is why you've done something and like it, without seeking the validation or approval of others. If you think it's unique, that's all that should really matter. Create first and foremost for yourself, no one else.

One of my passions is photography, and let me tell you, I take a lot of photos. Whether it's for social media, friends, family, or this book, it doesn't matter—I take them anytime and anywhere. One morning, I was out to breakfast with a friend and his entire family. We went to a little café in town on one of my many trips, and it was packed to the rafters. After waiting over an hour to get seven orders of scrambled eggs on toast with feta cheese, tomato, and avocado, the food arrived at our table. Immediately I noticed how beautifully this

breakfast was presented. So I whipped out my iPhone, stood on my chair, and began to take five to ten photos until the angle, light, and overall aesthetic were perfect. I could hear people around me giggling and could feel the eyes of strangers burning through my back like the hot summer sun. Did I care? Not at all. After several minutes of being the tallest person in the room, I got the shot I wanted, sat down, did some quick editing, and showed my peers what I'd come up with.

"WOW! That's beautiful," one of them said. And in the most humble way possible, I knew it was. More important, two minutes earlier, when I had stood on my chair looking like a complete idiot in front of an entire restaurant of strangers, I knew it would be. I knew it was going to be a cool picture and didn't care if I looked stupid taking it because I was led by my creative vision and not the opinions of others. I don't let other people control how I live my life.

When I get an idea, I roll with it, whatever the circumstances. I become obsessed with the thought, and it seeps into my every pore. I find it hard to put into words, but I get a kind of innovative high when I take a cool photo, film a particularly artistic video, or even just think of an inspirational idiom. I can't get enough of the act of creation. That visceral feeling pushes me forward.

My best friend, Troye, once told me, "If you wanna make cool shit, you gotta make cool shit," and it's engraved on my mind.

My creative process starts with an idea. I can't tell you for certain where it comes from. Ideas come to me in the shower, on airplanes, while I'm sitting in a restaurant, or lying in bed awake at 3:00 a.m., when my mind just can't seem to shut off. If it won't leave me alone, I begin expanding on it with notes. I think it all the way through, adding bullet points and examples. Then I just do it.

They don't always work out, and I'm okay with that. But when something does work out, I immediately show it to one of my closest friends to get feedback. I encourage critiques because I want it to be perfect before I put it out in the world. Once I make all the suggested changes that I agree with, I show everyone and soak up the positive remarks—and ignore the few hateful comments.

Ugh, I'm shaking a bit from pure excitement just typing about it. The experience is like no other for me.

What gives you that feeling? Everyone has something. Whatever it is, I can't encourage you enough to do that thing as soon—and as frequently—as possible. In life, you need to allow yourself the room to do what you want to do with the precious time you're given. Give yourself permission. I'm still young, but I often find myself thinking, "Ah! My time is ticking away! Why am I just sitting here doing nothing?" I need to use all the time I have, while I have it. After clearing that hurdle, you then have to actually do it, which is way more difficult than you might think. It's not easy breaking down barriers and not giving a single fuck about the opinions of others. Those opinions shouldn't inhibit your drive. Allow yourself to go there and add your splash of color to the world.

So, I'll ask you all again. Hands up if you want to be creative, take the risk, and embrace failure. I hope all your hands are in the air now.

The Chair

ALLOW ME TO TAKE YOU back to my philosophy classes as a freshman at college. Many of my friends had studied philosophy the first semester, drawing me into long conversations about life, making me question the simplest things and examine every possibility. I eat that stuff up. It never gets old. So one day in class, we were talking about upcoming exams and our professor said, "Let me tell you about an exam I took when I was in college."

He explained how, in one philosophy class, the teacher walked in, placed a chair at the front of the classroom, and said, "Explain to me why this isn't a chair." Then he left the room. That was the test: explain why the one thing in front of them wasn't what it appeared to be. After a lot of collective head scratching, the only kid who got an A was the boy who simply wrote on his paper, "What chair?"

The point is that a chair is a human-made object with a made-up label. It's not of nature, like a tree, a landscape, or a saltwater lake; it's something we as humans invented: we created and defined it. That story has stuck with me because it ties into my personal philosophy about the nature of things. People look at a chair and say, "It's just a chair," but I like to think it's more than a chair. I like to seek deeper meaning in things, even inanimate things. I know this makes me sound like a complete nutcase, but (a) I swear I'm not, and (b) it's just an example. Let me dive in further.

When people look at my photography and inquire about how I took a good picture, I tell them it's about stepping back and looking at the finer details and not taking things at face value. Life is about looking beneath the surface and seeing what lies beyond appearances.

That's not just a potted plant you see. Look closely; there's way more to it. Try looking at it from a different angle or maybe in a different light. Get up close and see its texture. Or the single drop of morning dew on its leaf. Or the beetle hiding among the flowers. Or the design on the pot. I wonder how those markings got there. I wonder who painted it and where it came from.

If you adopt a philosophical approach to things like that—always inquiring and going deeper—you may find more meaning in everything around you. Everything is worth a second glance.

I seek to look at the world through a new lens. Go on; give it a try. Look around you, wherever you are right now. What's the first thing that catches your eye? What's it made out of? Hmm, I wonder who chose that material. Where is it from? Wow! It came from thousands of miles away. What a journey that one little thing has been through.

You see? Anything you observe contains a story of interest, hidden behind a mask of simplicity. Looking at life this way forces you to appreciate your surroundings and helps you to understand that there's more to everything than meets the eye. With this mind-set, maybe you'll see the world a bit differently now.

The Fault in Our Scars

O NE NIGHT, WHEN I was eight years old, I accidentally rolled off my bed after tossing and turning in a sleep-filled daze. The unfortunate aspect of this middle-of-the-night tumble was that my bed sat a mere six inches away from the dresser. A solid, wooden dresser. With sharp edges. My face hit said dresser, leaving me with a black-and-blue bump that remains to this day on my forehead, dead center, just above my eyebrows. It's a scar I've carried through life, and I loathe it. Like a dent on the hood of a car, it's the first thing I see when I look in the mirror. Every. Single. Morning. Obviously there are wayyyyy worse things I could have wrong with me physically, and I shouldn't complain. But I'm letting you in here and admitting to an insecurity that's exacerbated in my line of work because my face is constantly on screen and available for the judgment of others. Sometimes I feel like the camera might as well be a large magnifying glass.

But we all carry scars that we have to deal with. This particular scar happens to be on the outside, but I have plenty on the inside as well, invisible to others. In fact, I'm willing to bet many people carry invisible scars. The scar of not being loved. The scar of verbal and mental abuse. The scar of abandonment. The scar of being taunted endlessly on the playground. The scar that heartbreak leaves behind. These invisible scars speak to a private struggle that very few of us dare to voice.

I'll let you in on a secret: I'm not perfect. Ohhh, shocker! It's easy to make it seem that way online, but I'm very insecure at times. My invisible scars mostly revolve around just wanting to be liked and to fit in. My whole life, all I wanted to do was be like everyone else and have everyone like me. I just wanted friends. I just wanted people to talk to me who appreciated me. And even to this day, as hard as I try, I still find myself sitting alone on my couch on some weekends with no invites to hang out. And when I do allow myself to be vulnerable and open with others, I never feel the emotions are reciprocated. With some "friends" I've had lately, it's a bit like walking down a one-way street that doesn't lead me anywhere I want to be.

But scars—inside and out—are only a big deal if we choose to focus on them and ignore the good things. I don't want to trivialize the causes of some of the most damaging scars that a person could carry, but in my experience, if you let your scars own you, they will. Don't give them that power. Don't let them stunt your growth and progress.

What I've learned to do with the scar I carry on the outside—the one everyone can see—is switch my perspective. It's not a scar to me anymore; it's a unique marking and part of my identity. If your scar is invisible, I encourage you to either embrace or confront it. Don't ig-nore it. Scars are daily reminders about something that happened to

us—usually something significant. We should appreciate their presence, or at least acknowledge them and look at them in a different way. There's nothing more inspiring than someone showing you a scar, telling you the story behind it, and letting you know he or she has accepted it and healed from it. I know I'd love to be able to do the same thing for each of my scars.

Someday.

If I Had an Art Installation

It's 8:00 p.m. I'm on a date. The engrossing topic at hand? Art installations. Art is all around us, so any chance I get to talk about its endless depths, I'll take. You see, I'm wildly obsessed with art.

After watching the documentary *The Artist Is Present* earlier this year, I had a particular fascination with that concept. In the film, the subject created an installation that involved herself, a table, two chairs, and an open invitation to anyone who wanted to join her at the table. And so it was that the question arose between me and my date: "If you could make an art installation, what would you create?"

With that, a thought immediately popped into my mind. I would create an exhibit that involved a room filled with people of all ages, shapes, sizes, and ethnicities, standing still. Completely naked.

The person viewing the exhibit would have to walk through a maze of bodies, making his or her way to the exit (taking whatever path he or she chose), along the way, viewing every type of person in his or her true form and thus an exposure to the rawness that is humanity stripped bare. In so doing—without the shield of fashion or the social masks we wear—each exhibitor is seen for who he or she truly is, and we get to see the reality that we are all individually unique, which is nothing short of beautiful. There is no hiding place. It's as real as it gets. It's art mirroring life.

Flawful

PEOPLE ARE BEAUTIFUL. All people, of all shapes and sizes. The fact that we are living, breathing organisms that happen to have opposable thumbs, allowing us to pick up our phone and be on it for the entire damn day, is nothing short of brilliant. What makes us even more magnificent as a species is that we are lucky enough to be uniquely different—and it's THAT individuality we must each harness and celebrate.

We're all pretty much stuck with what we've got appearance-wise, but more often than not, we fail to see our uniqueness as a good thing; instead, our differences lead us to make comparisons, with various likes and dislikes thrown in. Self-image can be daunting, especially when measured against our peers and the posters or photographs that the media project; it's hard to accept who we are, with all our imperfections. I know how it feels because I have struggled with looking in that mirror and not being fully satisfied with what I see. We can be our worst, and harshest, critics.

I was about eight years old when I first fixated on something about my looks that I didn't like.

"Mom?" I asked timidly as I ran into my parents' bedroom one evening, wiping tears from my cheeks.

"Hey, sweetie, what's wrong?" she asked.

Minutes earlier, I had gotten into a stupid fight with my older brother, Dustin. I can't remember what it was what about—probably something to do with a video game or who got the remote control while watching TV. (Oh, the power the remote provided when growing up.) I must have won our fight because my brother's low blow of a response was hard and fast: "Well, at least I'm not fat!!"

Ouch. I remember the sting those words left—like a football to the face in the middle of winter. An uncontrollable stream of tears formed quickly, and I turned and ran up the stairs to find Mom.

"Am I fat?" I asked.

"Honey," she said, sympathetically, "do you think you're fat?"

Until my brother had said it out loud, I hadn't really thought about it. Well, maybe a little. But his jab had vocalized that fleeting thought of mine.

"I don't know!" I replied, confused, triggering the tears once more. "Maybe."

Mom was quick to console me and eager to remove all judgment from the equation. "Well," she said, "if you think that, are you okay with it?"

In my worked-up state, I didn't know what to think. "I think so," I sniffled.

Then she came out with a pearl of wisdom that has always stuck with me: "If you like you, that's all that matters. If you don't, then maybe you could work out why that is."

And that, ladies and gentlemen, is why my mom is the best. Somebody give that woman a mother-of-the-year trophy, stat!

I find it so interesting that for a period in everyone's life, we are completely innocent: no worries, no troubles, barely a care in the world. Wouldn't it be nice if we could harness that carefree spirit and walk through life in its protective bubble? I bet it's nice never to worry. I can't recall the last time I didn't have something keeping me wide awake at night. When we're kids, the biggest thing we have to worry about is whether we want white or chocolate milk at lunch. Those were the days. (Yet again I sound like I'm an middle-aged adult. *rolls eye at self*)

Anyway, I decided to ask a couple of friends how old they were when they first found something about themselves they didn't like. Each had the same response: "I was between eight and ten."

I'm never going to look at a kid in that age range the same way again. In my mind's eye, I see a small eight- to ten-year-old child and I think, "Oh, you poor, poor thing. You're about to go through some rough patches, but it'll get better. But first, it gets so much worse." *pats child on head, walks away*

But this proves that we're all in this together, experiencing the same kind of insecurities, feeling similar things like self-doubt and self-judgment. Sure, some guys and girls are better at concealing it than others, but those same negative thoughts go through our heads when they stand in front of the mirror naked or walk into a crowded classroom after the bell. Confidence and smiles are just the masks we learn to wear from a young age; maybe we allow those masks to fall with our close friends and family because they're the only people with whom we can truly be ourselves.

To this day, I still don't like every single thing about my appearance. I constantly flash back to my childhood weight issues or ponder the bump on my forehead, my slight underbite, the awkward amount of hair on my body, and too many other things. To be honest, it can be exhausting at times.

Raise your hand if you like every single aspect of your appearance. Unless Beyoncé is reading this book, there should be no hands in the air. (And if Beyoncé is reading this, then, um, heyyyyyyyy, Queen Bey!! *smiles and waves like a madman*)

It's normal to grow up and dislike things about ourselves. It's human. It's what discovering our individuality is all about. All of us overmagnify our self-perceived flaws, be it a scar from falling out of a bed, a birthmark, a zit, a not-so-classic facial feature, or the general shape of our figure. But if we all ran around as perfect, plastic clones, then the world would be a boring, bleak place. The "flaws" we carry are all part and parcel of our uniqueness. But let me tell you something: *no one else cares about your flaws.* Truly, I'm saying this in the nicest, kindest way: no one notices them but you. It's all in your head.

I'm always shocked to learn that most people don't notice the bump on my forehead because to me, it protrudes like a freaking lighthouse, sending an SOS signal to everyone in the general vicinity. I've even been told that this "flaw" is cute. CUTE. Apparently others adore about me the thing I hate most.

And there lies my point: once we learn to accept who we are, imperfections and all, then—and only then—can we achieve our full potential. Forget about negative self-image and self-judgment. It's about self-love, and no one teaches you that at school. No one teaches you that if you accept and love yourself, nothing and no one can touch you.

This is the only face and body you're ever going to get, so be comfortable and happy in it. Own it. Own every aspect of who you are and present it to the world with the utmost pride.

Numb to the Numbers

THE SOCIAL GENERATION has taken over. If you don't tweet on the daily, receive dozens of likes on Instagram photos, and know what the heck Tumblr is, then you best get to Googling because you've been left behind.

Or you're, like, forty. It seems that every person in our ever-connected world is on some form of social media. (If you're one of the few who isn't, I applaud you. Stay. Away. That shit is more addictive than a fresh jar of Nutella on a lonely Friday evening.) Our lives are never offline, and we're permanently logged in. One foot in the moment, one foot somewhere else entirely. In this cyber-reality—one in which we can now wear and carry our computers at all times—it's difficult not to get caught up in the bubble of "likes," thumbs-ups, ratings, comments, and general Internet chatter—and therein lies THE TRAP for our self-esteem. The trap that awaits us all: the importance of being liked.

As a generation, we seem to glean a sense of validation from the numbers, for reasons I don't entirely understand. I read somewhere that a popular post or photo rewards us with a rush of endorphins—

hence the addiction. It's science, people. Don't deny it. What's clear is that the higher the number of likes—or retweets—the better the feeling. But the importance attached to it is false. None of us should measure our self-esteem or popularity by numbers. Social media is the most warped mirror to look into.

I'm the first to admit that I'm over the moon if I receive over 100,000 likes on a YouTube video. Hitting that number makes me feel that I've created content that's pretty darn good and something I should be proud of. When I stop to truly think about it, that's a huge number of clicks! Think about it: 100,000 unique people watched my video and decided it worthy of taking two extra seconds to move their mouse cursor over the little green thumbs-up button and . . . CLICK! That's incredible to me.

But, you know what? I don't even know those people, and that's the reality check I had to give myself a long time ago. Yes, I remember when my first 50 likes meant something, but after a while, the numbers—from 100 to 100,000 to 1 million to infinity and beyond—became figures without meaning, and I'm happy it's gotten to that point. A number doesn't validate who I am or what I'm doing.

Not that I'm immune to the trap. If I get only ten likes on a personal Facebook post, that sucks! Like, wow, okay, none of my REAL friends thought my photo was cute, or that status was hilarious, or my birthday was worthy of a personal message. *sobs heavily*

But we should always check in with ourselves and maintain a grip on reality. Same with taking selfies. "It's okay to take selfies all the time," I've heard it said, "because that means you're happy with the way you look and want to show people you're confident." I couldn't agree more. But you also risk seeming self-indulgent and egotistical. You risk measuring your self-worth by the number of likes you receive. Here's the bottom line: if you're truly confident, you don't need to seek the likes of others. And if you're not so confident, then fuel your self-esteem with the love of your friends and family.

It's okay to want to be liked. It's okay to seek likes. But it's not okay if you allow those likes to become the foundation of your sense of self-worth, because other people might not be putting a whole lot of thought into the process of liking—or not liking—your photos or posts. Remember that likes are just numbers—they don't add anything to your personal value. I know it's easy to get wrapped up in it all, but take it from someone who has experienced all levels of appreciation: None of it matters.

The best way to avoid falling into the trap is to stop paying attention to the likes. Take the photo. Post the video. Tweet the tweet. And that's it. Don't look back and let the number, high or low, make you feel any better or worse. It's a vicious cycle that you don't want to get caught up in. Have confidence in yourself and what you put out into the world.

Be numb to the numbers. Don't let the numbers numb you.

Say No

No. NO. nO. Noooooooo. no.

No matter how I say it, saying "no" is difficult for me. That word doesn't strike my vocal cords naturally, especially when I don't want to do something or go somewhere. My mind is saying *NO!* but I can't get myself to say it out loud. It's probably because I'm a people pleaser—too concerned with being polite and not letting people down instead of honoring my true wishes. It seems I'd rather do something I don't enjoy than have someone I'm with have a poor time or be upset with me. That said, I'm determined to overcome this block. I'm learning slowly that the world won't end if I utter that scary two-letter word. People won't hate me. Things won't crumble to pieces. In fact, the honesty may be appreciated and a compromise will most likely be found.

So, here, say it out loud with me: NO.

Wait, I Just Need to Check Something . . .

So EVERYONE'S AGREED: we're all a little too obsessed with technology. In fact, I'm willing to bet my left pinky toe that you have a phone on your person right this second.

Did I win the bet?

Yup, that's what I thought. Our phones have become another limb, it seems. "Oops, we need to go back! Forgot my phone!" or "Can we wait a couple minutes while my phone charges? I don't want it to die while we're out." I hear such things on a daily basis, uttered in the kind of tone that hints at fear and separation anxiety. Why is it that we can't do *anything* without bringing this little computer box with us?

Being a child of the digital age, it's difficult for me to question this habit because, frankly, I fucking love my phone. I'm guilty of being glued to mine all the time. I'm not much better than the next person. But here's the thing: I am *aware* of how overly attached I've become, and, since acknowledging this issue, I've gotten better.

One of my favorite things to do when at dinner with friends is to play the "all phones in the center of the table" game. Basically, everyone turns their phones on silent and places them in the no-touching zone on the table. The first person to reach out and use it must pay for dinner. Works like a charm, because, out of pure economic fear, no one ever grabs their cell first. OH, THE HUMANITY!

The beauty of this enforced phone withdrawal is that all techno-distractions are removed. We are compelled to interact and communicate directly with one another, and it's refreshing. As someone whose job is to be online 24/7, I savor the break from the virtual world. It's like, "Nope, can't reply for the next hour or two! I'm busy." Busy spending time with friends—quality, uninterrupted time.

But it's sad to think that this game even has to exist—to think people prefer to interact with those who aren't with them instead of the people right in front of them. I tend to yell at my friends when I see this happening: "I'm right here! Put your phone down!" I say. "Whoever you're talking to will be there when we're done."

We should all speak up when someone's attention leaves us. But it's an addiction. I get it. Psychologists get it too. That's why they've named this addiction "nomophobia"—an abbreviation for no-mobile-phone phobia. A study in Britain in 2014 found that 53 percent of phone users feel trembling anxiety if they "lose their phone, run out of battery or credit, or have no network coverage."

I think it's more of an addiction to being social, and our phones are the enablers of that. Yet they incredibly inhibit our social skills, thwarting the art of conversation. Who knows if this pattern of behavior will help or hurt us in the long run?

I'm learning to prevent it more and more every day by just being

more aware of when I'm on my phone. When an in-person conversation seems to be ending, I think up a new question to keep it going instead of reaching for my phone in preparation for the potential awkwardness ahead. If I'm hanging out with someone, I'll put my phone on silent and look at only after that person has left. If I'm at home, I'll leave my phone in the other room "to charge" in hopes that I won't miss or think twice about it.

Turns out, all of these techniques work and no one dies when I don't pay attention to my phone 24/7! WHO KNEW??? Strange to think the online world can wait a minute while you live your life.

The choice is ours: engage with real life or escape into a virtual world. Do you want to communicate with living, breathing people right in front of you? Or wait until some lifeless words pop up on a screen? You decide which is more fulfilling.

I know my preference.

Coffee

On the wall above the stove in my kitchen is a sign that declares, "Coffee Made Me Do It." This not only sums up my love for the beverage, it also allows me to mention the great difference between the act of drinking coffee and the true purpose of it.

I don't drink it for the caffeine most of the time. I simply enjoy the act and full-bodied experience that comes from savoring it. Many coffee drinkers need two cups daily to keep 'em going. I've never felt that way. And I can't do what the Italians do: order, knock it back, and go. To me, that ruins the whole thing.

The purpose of coffee for me is to set the tone for the rest of my day. When I wake up, it's part of my routine to ensure I allow myself enough time to carefully brew a fresh pot of deliciousness. That way, I can sit down, catch up on Internet things, e-mails, and texts and mentally prepare for the day. It is also personal and social—it can mean "me time" or, if I'm with a friend, "we time." The act of drinking coffee soothes and relaxes. The caffeine is just a bonus in my book. Now you know why I often take artsy photos wherever and whenever I find myself indulging in, enjoying, and relaxing with my favorite beverage. Because coffee made me do it.

Connor likes his bugs

Connor Franta, Hokah Chiefs

I have been in entomology for two years. Entomology is the study of bugs or insects. I have over one hundred different bugs in my collection. I went to state last year with my bug collection. It was a great experience.

When I first started bug collecting I didn't know anything about it, but now I know a lot about it. I had to learn the categories in which the bugs went in. That was probably the hardest to memorize. When I find new bugs, I look them up in my bug book to see what it's called. Then I have to make a label for the bug.

I catch the bugs by just using a

Connor Franta

butterfly net. After you catch the bugs, you need to freeze them in the freezer. Whenever you have time later, you get them out of the freezer and put a pin through the middle of the body. If it is a butterfly or moth, you spread its wings out. If it is a beetle, you spread its legs out. Then you let them dry for a week.

Whenever you have time you go anywhere outside and look all over for new bugs. When I find a new bug, I am really happy. My favorite thing to collect is probably butterflies and moths. They come in all different shapes, sizes, and colors. I recommend bug collecting to everyone because it is very exciting.

The Problem with Labels

FIGURING OUT WHO WE ARE is what life is all about—the Holy Grail. That seems to be what everyone of all ages is seeking. In this search for identity, I've found that one thing tends to get in the way: labels. A label—a classifying phrase or name applied to a person or thing that tells us what it is—is an attempt at a definition. But more often than not, society's labels can be inaccurate, narrow, or restrictive. Labels are too confining. We humans are complex beings; we cannot be simply categorized.

I never want to feel that I'm an inaccurate portrayal of myself or restricted from reaching my full potential. I'm also a lot of things, not just one. Take the label "YouTuber," which is used to describe me all the time. I embrace the fact that I'm a YouTuber and am very proud of it, but it's not all that I am. It puts me in a box and provides context. And okay, in one word, it explains what I do, but that doesn't, and shouldn't, define my existence or tell you who I am. But I'll guarantee you this: when you mention "YouTuber" to a bunch of strangers who are, say, in their thirties or beyond, you don't have to wait and watch

long before the snap judgments follow. Go on, try it: "Connor's a You-Tuber . . ."

Age is another example of a label you can never really escape, but is extremely defining: "You're too young to do that" or "You're way too old for that." Those are things we've all heard from time to time, and they never cease to be annoying. At twenty-two years old, I'm not a kid anymore, but I tend to be treated like one in many work-related situations. I could easily say, "Yes, I may still be young, but I'm very wise for my age and have a lot to say!" But that rarely works. They only way for a kid to be taken seriously and treated as an equal by someone more experienced is to prove it. Prove you have something to say. Prove you are doing something beyond your years. And for me, that's what I try to do: Prove them wrong. You can too.

From an early age, I have struggled with labels. I realized that I found it hard to self-identify with any one thing. Am I a jock, a nerd, or a popular kid? Am I the good kid or the rebel? Do I like boys, girls, or both? It was all very stressful and tiring because such questions played a huge role in how I saw myself and how others perceived me—and that terrified me deeply. I even wondered if people were going to judge me because maroon was, and remains, my favorite color. Is it too feminine a color? If so, what does that say about me?

Society's need for labels is why, at some time or another, we have all postured in the shop window of social media to invent or uphold a certain image that we think is "cool" or "relatable" or "perfect," so that everyone on the outside looking in gets the impression we want to leave. First impressions are important, after all. Yet aren't the majority of us wary of the labels people so easily and inaccurately apply to us, be they racial, ethnic, or sexual? Isn't that also why many of us obsess about the literal labels we wear on our clothes, because the brands are supposed to represent that we are cool, fashionable, or even wealthy?

In fact, labels gloss over who we actually are. They plaster over the cracks and create a smooth image that does not allow us the freedom to be our true selves. When I am asked certain categorizing questions—and I get them daily—I'm reluctant to pick one response because I'm wary of what that one response will say about me. Do I say my favorite book is *The Fault in Our Stars* or Walter Isaacson's

biography of Steve Jobs? I love both books, but what kind of conclusions will people jump to depending on what I say?

That's what labels do—they provide a launch pad for judgment. However people view you, there will be times when you will be judged, often harshly and wrongly. And it will be based on what you do, wear, or like and the friends you hang around with. If you're highly intelligent, you'll be "an overachiever." If you're incredibly kind, you'll be "a goody-goody." If you're a little shy and quiet, you'll be "boring" or "awkward." But trust me, the judgment says more about the labeler than the labeled.

As I said earlier, life is all about figuring out who we are. We are constantly growing, learning, and changing as people, and I love that. Honestly, I could barely recognize the person I saw in the mirror a year ago if I saw him today. I want to be able to keep saying that through life.

So let other people apply the labels, but don't let that label become your straitjacket. In fact, use the opportunity to take those labels and redefine them. Enhance it. Expand on it. Break through the barriers and limitations. Carve out an identity that is unique to you. Don't agree to be marked, filed, and put into a box that will hinder your true potential.

Who are you?

Answer: You are who you are in this given moment. Label-less. Limitless.

Remember that from this day forward.

A Person Worth Ignoring
Your Phone For

I T'S A DAY LIKE ANY other. The sun is shining, kids are swinging on the swings and playing kickball on the playground, and I'm with my friend Taylor, a fellow first grader, sitting at the back of the school building. We're talking about life, global warming, politics, and our hope that there will be macaroni and cheese for lunch—you know, the usual six-year-old stuff.

Taylor, being the little troublemaker she is, asks if I want to go down to the dumpster; she has something to show me. So we venture down to the secluded, smelly area and stop behind a container holding garbage. *This better be good, Taylor,* I think. *This place stinks.*

"You ever been kissed before?" she asks brazenly, with a mischievous look in her eyes behind her cute, round glasses—almost as cute as the jeans and T-shirt she's wearing.

I immediately feel my cheeks blush. "Um, what? Uh, no?"

"You want to try it?" she asks, a little forcefully. Typical Tay.

"Um, okay," I say, completely unsure. "I think so."

She closes her eyes and leans in. I mimic her. Our lips touch, and then we both quickly pull away. Our eyes dart open and we look at each other—half embarrassed, half shocked—before giggling and running off in different directions. Once out of sight, once I've stopped running, I gather my infantile thoughts. *I think I'm in love*, I tell myself.

Whatever that means.

I wish I could say that matters of the heart become easier as we get older, but whether you're six, ten, fourteen, eighteen, or twenty-one, love—or what we think is love—is capable of reducing us all to children. It's truly an indescribable feeling that you won't understand until it hits you, rendering you out of control and feeling all sorts of irrational things. We're all struck dumb by the spell it casts over us. I don't get it. But I like it.

Love is complicated. Anyone who's felt it, whether fleeting or lasting, will tell you the same thing. You never see it coming until, BOOM, it smacks you right in the face like a football. (Or something. Maybe not like that. I hate football, so I wouldn't know, but I imagine you're never expecting its impact—or for it to hurt.) What I'm trying to say is that love is unpredictable, capable of striking from any direction. I mean, Taylor snuck up on me behind a dumpster! How more unpredictable can it get?!

But going beyond first grade, it has been the same for me ever since. I didn't plan on it. I barely even sought out relationships. One day, this person was just there and I was thrown completely off guard.

My first relationship was with a girl named Carlye. She was petite, beautiful, and bubbly. We were on the cross-country team together and it was love at the first 5K. Okay, maybe not "love," but I was smit-

ten, to say the least, I think. I mean, I was, like, twelve. *She's very pretty and nice*, I thought when her friend told me, "Carlye likes you!"

Very subtle, friend.

"Yeah, I think I like her, too," I replied, shyly.

She walked back to Carlye and her other friends, and they all giggled. And just like that, I had my first girlfriend. Kinda.

Dating is strange when you're in your preteen and teen years, and this new relationship consisted of awkward conversations, hanging out in groups, holding hands, and, well, that was about it. But regardless of how little we actually did, it all seemed very heavy. Everything felt new. Everything felt as if it was life or death. This was huge! Kinda.

We ended up being together for maybe two months—short-lived, to say the least, but I didn't really feel anything anyway.

On the cusp of adolescence, I was in my experimental years, making my first, tentative ventures into the minefield of relationships. Expect a long road ahead, my friends. Because when we expose our fledgling emotions to the blazes of love, we tend to run headlong into the fire, lured by the excitement it promises.

Relationships *are* fire—they're about chemistry. No spark, no go. Once you find someone you find visually pleasing, you pursue him or her. If you discover that you also enjoy this person's personality, interests, and company and the feeling is mutual, you move to dating. If you're lucky enough for that to go well, you take it a step further and make it official. Congratulations! You're in a relationship with a real person! NICE!

These three basic steps may sound simple and easy, but if you've ever made a real attempt at them, you'll find otherwise. Love is hard. *Really* hard! And in this day and age, everything seems a bit more difficult, probably because we're surrounded by constant distractions, not to mention phones, tablets, laptops, social media, texts, photos, and more. We have a constant stream of information right at the tips of our fingers.

That is power. That is a problem.

I cannot tell you how many times I've been around people who seem more interested in their phones than my company. What am I, a brick wall??? SPEAK TO ME, HUMAN!

Thankfully, the majority of people I've been with seem to have an awareness of etiquette and when to put the phone down, though I've witnessed people succumbing to that easy distraction on first dates. How rude. How unnecessary. I don't envy the kids younger than me who are born into this technological era and will forever have to live with its madness.

My worst date ever involved forgetting my wallet and having to drive back home in silence and sadness (she comforted me, saying it was no big deal, but I felt otherwise). But forgetting your wallet is one thing; forgetting your social skills is another, and totally unforgivable. Don't know where you can find an extra set of those.

I'm traditional at heart. I don't use apps to find dates and don't like being on my phone around other people (unless it's people I don't know, then, ew, no, I hate socializing with strangers.) I also prefer phone calls to texting, walking to driving, and casual to formal. I look forward to deep conversations and never want a stupid phone to get in the way. Your date deserves your undivided attention. If you don't give it, well, that person can't be that special to you. It's best to hang out with the person you're texting instead.

This strict stance didn't come naturally to me at first. It took a lot of experience and observation—and self-awareness—before I changed my ways. I realized what I was doing, saw others behaving the same way, and corrected myself. But, you know by now, that's how I acquire a lot of my knowledge: observing myself and others.

But back to dating. Here's what I've learned: you need to enjoy another person so much that you want to be around that person as much as you're around yourself. That sounds crazy, almost like a potential death wish. Most people can barely handle being around themselves 24/7, let alone another living, breathing human being. But when you find someone who makes all of that seem completely sane, you've got a keeper.

My first real relationship that wasn't some high school fling wasn't until my freshman year of college when, at orientation, I attended a dance with my new friend Ricky. We walked into the loud reception area and spotted one of his old friends across the room. And standing next to the friend was a girl named Bailey. We instantly hit it off and dated for nine months—months that were filled with many firsts for me. Suffice it to say that I got to experience what it's like to deeply and romantically care for another person; to be close, to be intimate, to be in a functioning relationship. Yet in the end, I felt nothing, almost as if I was going through the motions of something. I didn't feel this "love" thing that people talked about. I didn't see it in Bailey's face. I didn't sense it in my heart, and that was daunting, to say the least. All I truly felt was a mass of confusion—and this was the beginning of understanding who I was. It continued into my late teens, and each time a relationship broke down, heartbreak wasn't something I felt. *Something* was missing, and it was hard to ignore that inescapable instinct that I should be feeling something more, something deeper.

At the time, I put it down to the fact that meeting the right person was difficult. Just ask your parents. Love, and especially the maintenance of love, takes much work. Love is about sitting in silence and enjoying every second of it simply because your partner is sharing it with you. Love is about reading another person's mind and finishing his or her sentences—because you know that person that well. Love is about wanting to be as physically close as possible because you can't get enough of the other's smell, feel, or mere presence. Love is about putting another person before yourself because, quite simply, when that person is happy, you're happy. Love is about staying in on the weekend, ordering Indian food, and putting on a new documentary because you wouldn't want to be with anyone else. Love knows no gender, race, shape, or size. Love is love—an energy that fuses souls. And when you fall into its warm embrace, you won't want to let go.

'That's what love is to me. 'That's the standard I hold, and I can clearly see a person in my mind that fills the mold. Can you? If not, keep looking. That love is out there. It exists and finds us all. And I hope you all find that one person who makes you want to ignore your phone and get lost in his or her company. That person is waiting for you (or maybe you have already found him or her).

Live Now, Worry Later

BASED ON THE LAST YEAR alone, I never would have guessed that this is where I would be. I think back to all those times I worried about what path to take and what I wanted to do, and look what happened—life guided me to where I was destined to be. *Destiny* and *destin*ation share a root word for good reason.

I recently read this quote : "Worry is the interest on a debt that may never become payable." It made me realize how much time I have wasted needlessly worrying about outcomes I can't control. Life is always going to keep us guessing; often it throws us for a complete loop. But that's the fun part. The uncertainty—the not knowing—*is* the adventure. What would be the point of life if things were con-stantly black-and-white and predictable; if we knew from the begin-ning where we'd ultimately end up? I would despise that. Yet many of us are so caught up in regrets or worries rooted in past experience and so fretful of looking into an unknown future that we lose sight of what's happening here and now.

Ever since I was young, I've been a bit of a worrywart. I worried about what other people were doing or saying, being included, my grades, my future, what I wanted for lunch, which TV channel to watch . . . you know, the usual. It has been the bane of my existence, that strong need to constantly know what was going to unfold. It stressed me out to think that every single decision could dramatically alter my life in a good or bad way—or nothing could happen. I found myself listing the endless "what-ifs" in my head, attempting to determine every outcome.

As an adult, I find myself worrying about similar things, but now I also have much bigger—and more important—things to worry about. I worry if I'm doing my taxes right, if I paid that bill, if I should have insurance for this or that, if my career doesn't work out. Real people things. Very scary real people things.

Thankfully, I'm now better at managing all this ruminating, understanding that my past is simply a memory, replaced day by day by the present. By living in the now, I'm creating a bright future ahead. "Live now, worry later" is my new mantra.

I often hear people say things like, "Take me back to when I was younger. It was better then!" or, "I just want this point in my life to be over. Things will be so much better later on!" The underlying theme is being BACK THEN or LATER ON, to which I say, "What about right freaking now, huh?"

You can't change the past. It's done. Finished. Unless time travel becomes real, you best deal with what you have now. The future is both unknown and unseen—you're trying to control the invisible. How pointless is that?! We waste so much time, energy, and emotion on the uncontrollable. No wonder worry can be so exhausting.

Instead, we should think about how incredible it is that each of us

has a gloriously uncertain future ahead. Destination unknown. It's like being in a movie where you don't know the end. Think of it that way.

Take it from someone who has changed his mind-set: you can make "now" the place you want to be. Rub your eyes, focus, and see what's right in front of you: the gift of life. What you do with that gift is up to you. If you want to sit around all day tweeting about how much you hate your life and can't wait until you're older, I wish you well. But why wait!! You could ACT NOW. What's holding you back? (If you're a teenager, don't you dare say "school." You can work around that to build toward the future, so no excuses.)

None of us wants our existence to be based on what-ifs. So in the spirit of our collective interest, I suggest that you too shift your focus. Stop looking over your shoulder. Stop looking off into the distance. Stop dwelling on expectations. Simply take stock and concentrate on how you feel and what you need right now. Then do it! Every decision you take today is a building block for the future that awaits you. As Joseph Campbell once said, "We must let go of the life we have planned, so as to accept the one that is waiting for us."

So what are you waiting for? Let go, my friend.

Respect for My Elders

I was at a family's party recently and decided to spend the evening talking with the host's grandmother. Well dressed, with white hair, she had a spitfire personality, and as we sat in a corner, we discussed her life: where she's lived, what memories she treasures, what she's learned. We even talked about how she cooked a delicious casserole—and who I should kill in order to get the recipe! Throughout the entire conversation, I was fascinated by her story of a life well lived.

This is something you need to know about me: eleven times out of ten, I would rather talk to an eighty-seven-year-old than an eighteen-year-old. I gravitate toward wisdom. And the elderly are just so freaking cute, I can't resist! People of age have been through it all and have a rich collection of stories to share. And if we take the time, pull up a chair, let them talk, and really listen, we can learn a thing or two. Respect those who have been here before us. They've walked the path. They know the way.

The Long Road to Me

YOU MIGHT THINK FINDING YOURSELF is tough and ends in high school. I wish that were true. Finding yourself is a lifelong journey. Just when you think you know who you are, life has this way of throwing a curveball and landing you back in the town of confusion; population: a vast majority of the human race.

Everyone's path to self-discovery is bound to be different. Whatever decisions and directions we take, big and small, they all combine to help us figure out who we are. But at many crossroads, the confusion or indecision most of us will feel is part and parcel of the mystery of life. At times, you're going to wish you were someone else. On occasion, you're going to be tempted to look back. But until you find your way, all I can recommend is that you keep moving forward, even when the fog has descended and the destination is unknown.

I don't speak as some wise old wizard on the hill. I speak as someone who has experienced the utter, head-spinning confusion surrounding the core of my identity. The needle on my personal compass was always doing a 360, spinning out on the determination of my sexuality. For much of my twenty-two years, I struggled quietly with that part of myself.

What follows is my story.

* * *

From a young age, I always felt something was different about me, without being able to put my finger on it. I'm not saying I had this sixth sense as a toddler, but my individuality was on display 24/7. Adults constantly told my parents how "energetic, talkative, and dramatic" I was, or they commented on my "big personality for someone so young." Of course, I never thought anything about these traits because, well, I was a fetus. Why would people gawking over me provide anything but a feel-good factor? Who doesn't love that kind of attention?! (This was long before my homecoming king days.)

It wasn't until I turned twelve that my perspective changed. I began to see differences between me and other boys. I noticed that they weren't as animated. As I got older, a lot of kids mentioned that gay people acted the way I did, which was bewildering and scary to hear because of the negative connotation associated with being gay. I began to check myself, holding back my personality to put distance between me and the stereotype. I censored my actions and words out of fear of what I could be.

But then I started to think about it.

The question that popped into my head during seventh grade was, "What if I'm gay?" I don't know what sparked that random thought, that nudge from the inside. Maybe it was something I had seen on the Internet. Maybe it was a conversation with friends that triggered something deep. Maybe it was just a little boy questioning the world around him as puberty dawned. Who knows? But one

thing's for sure: I thought about it. I mean, I REALLY thought about it. That one, terrifying self-inquiry quickly engulfed my mind. Terror was the overriding emotion—fear that I was something I knew nothing about; scared that I was somehow a freak for even thinking such a thing. I tried to push the thought away, desperate to think of something—anything—else, but my mind clung to it like a magnet, unable to separate from its force. Sleepless nights became frequent, and would carry on for years. I cast all my confusion up to the ceiling, staring, wide awake. Worse than that, the self-judgment and self-hatred kicked in for daring to think such taboo things.

As a kid from a small town in the Midwest, being gay wasn't common in my experience; at least, no one openly talked about it. I didn't know anyone who was gay, and I'd never had a conversation with another person, or my family, about gay people. All I sensed was that it wasn't seen as a good thing. My parents had never mentioned the subject, so I didn't know what their opinion would be either. What if they hated it too?

That was why I decided not to say anything. I never told a soul, preferring to bottle everything up and not give voice to this instinct screaming inside me. No one could know. If someone knew, then those thoughts could become something real, something I had to deal with. As a result, I became sad and felt very alone, that way most of us do when we have convinced ourselves that we're the odd one out. This silent misery continued until I moved into my high school years, and that was when I decided the only solution—the only way to be "normal"—was not to be gay. Simple, right?

I tried what most teenage boys do: date girls. This pretense wasn't too difficult to adopt. "Yes, she's pretty," I'd say if someone asked me about a certain girl I had been hanging out with. "So are you a 'thing'?" they'd ask, intrigued to know more. "Well, she's nice, we have fun so, um, maybe we will be?" I would say, caving in to the pressure.

That was how it often played out. I went along with the lie—the lie to myself, my friends, the girls—and kept dating. When things got a little serious, I made up some bogus reason to back out. "I don't have enough time" and "I'm really trying to focus on athletics" were excuses I used to end two relationships. Truth is, I felt nothing. The girls were nice and all, but they were into it and I wasn't, so I had to find an exit strategy. And then, in my last two years of high school, I told everyone, "I'm done dating for now. It's too much work—maybe later in life."

Years passed, and at college, I found myself interested in another girl. *Maybe she'll be the one who'll get these incessant "Am I gay?" thoughts out of my head,* I thought. But one night, when said girlfriend and I were making out, I remember my mind drifting. *Are we done yet? I'm so bored. How do people enjoy this??*

As you probably assumed, that relationship didn't work out. Even with the benefit of time, I couldn't like girls in *that* way—a realization that left me feeling the lowest I had ever felt. A sense of hopelessness was heaped onto all the confusion, and I began to accept that I was going to be the guy who'll never have relationships or get married, that bachelor guy who lives alone forever and dies. That, I convinced myself, was my bleak and lonely future, so I better get used to it.

At this point, I even went as far as posting a video to my YouTube channel, titled "I'm Not Gay." I had been receiving so many rude com-

ments about my sexuality that I figured an outright denial would put an end to it all. By posting something online, I could once and for all tell people that this is who I am, so quit asking. That public denial remained up there as a permanent shield to all the curiosity.

Now fast-forward two years, when I moved to Los Angeles.

The vast majority of people I met in Southern California were dreamers—ambitious, creative, and driven. Nothing could beat the year-round amazing weather, and my career was flourishing. Life couldn't have been going any better. From any outsider's perspective, I appeared to be the happiest I'd ever been. But in reality, it was the most miserable period of my life. That was because the thoughts in my head had somehow found a megaphone, screaming at me every minute of every day: "YOU LIKE BOYS! YOU ARE GAY! JUST SAY IT! WHAT ARE YOU WAITING FOR?!" And yet I still admitted nothing and kept it all in. Just another person maintaining a happy facade in Hollywood.

And then on the evening of January 3, 2014, I actually said it. Well, I said it to myself, but that self-admission felt like the biggest leap of my twenty-two-year existence. I don't know what sparked it in my mind, but I happened to be staring at myself, dead in the eyes, in the bathroom mirror. I held my own stare, watching the tears well and feeling my body start to quiver, and then shake, with both rage and terror. "I'm gay," I told my reflection, whispering it. "I am gay," I repeated, a little louder.

What happened next surprised even me: I smiled. Through all the pain, I actually smiled, feeling a sudden rush of relief, as if being freed from a choking grip. As if I had released my own hands from around my neck. I looked at myself in the mirror again and a smile

turned into a grin, the kind that greets an old friend. I was happy with the image reflected back at me.

I knew this was just the beginning of a breakthrough. Next, I needed to tell someone. I spent the next seven days trying to summon that courage. Then, on January 11, 2014, at 5:00 a.m., after keeping one of my friends up because I wanted to "just hang out," I said outright, to another person, for the first time: "I am gay."

His reaction was nothing short of great. Initially he seemed a bit shocked, but that almost instantaneously melted away and he switched into comforting mode. "You're okay and it will all be okay," he said, reassuringly. That was the day—the dawn—when I felt my life had truly begun. My friend's acceptance was liberating. I was free. I was the real me. And I was no longer afraid—at least, not as afraid as I had been.

From that point on, it was a case of finding the courage, and the right time, to tell more and more people. First, a few more friends; then my mom and dad, followed by more friends, siblings, and even more friends, until there was barely anyone left to tell. Mom conveniently came to visit California in the spring, and I knew I had to tell her. I had to tell her everything, although that didn't lessen the enormity of the task at hand. I waited until the last night when I was dropping her off at her hotel, all the time rehearsing the words in my head and feeling so incredibly nervous.

We pulled up outside the hotel, said goodnight, and she got out. But just before she could close the door, I said, "Mom, wait a sec!"

I hurriedly got out of the car and told her what I felt she needed to know. "Oh honey, it's okay," she said. "It doesn't matter to me. Are you seeing anyone?"

That part surprised me the most. She went past all the little details and was genuinely interested in knowing about the big picture. From that day on, we've been closer than we ever had been before.

As I dropped her off at the airport early the next morning, she asked if she could tell my dad because "I can't lie to your father." Within hours of getting home, I received a call from Mom and she said, "Hey, here's your dad."

Great, I thought. *I didn't expect this so soon!*

My dad had the same warm, accepting reaction, except he cried. And so did I. And then my mom. There were a lot of tears on that call, but once again, I felt better than ever. I proceeded to tell my sister over the phone, my older brother on Skype, and my little brother in person when I returned home for a summer visit. Each of them said the same thing: "It's okay, Con. I still love you."

They were all so great that I wished I'd told them earlier. Love trumps fear every time.

Once family and friends had all been checked off, I had only one more hurdle to clear: confessing it in public to my followers and fans on YouTube. My nerves are evident in that video, posted on December 8, 2014.

A lot of people wondered if I "really needed to post a video about it," and others asked, "Why does the world have to know? Isn't anything personal for you anymore?"

But that video was bigger than me. Okay, it was going to make me feel as "me" as I could be, but its wider purpose was to help others in a similar position. With a large audience, I often feel a certain sense of responsibility to guide, inform, and nurture whenever possible. I had been thinking about that video for a good month or two, waiting until it felt right to post.

I had actually filmed my coming-out video two days earlier but initially thought it was absolute shit. The lighting kept changing, leaf blowers could be heard in the background, and, overall, I felt like a nervous wreck. But I sat down, edited it, watched it again, and realized I was just being hard on myself. It was, in fact, exactly what I wanted it to be: raw, real, unscripted—and me. After two panic-filled days, I uploaded the video at 10:06 a.m. and watched with one hand over my eye as all the support flowed in. The feedback was truly overwhelming. The result was bigger than I ever thought it would be. I had needlessly worried about this whole thing for nothing and doubted the reactions of the people in my life.

My journey, and the evolving process of staying true to myself, won't stop there. I am, like everyone else, still figuring myself out on a daily basis. I surprise myself all the time by doing and accomplishing things I had never thought possible. But this path I've been walking is clearer than it has ever been. The fog has lifted, and the possibilities are endless. With nothing holding me back and by staying true to myself, I honestly feel there is nothing I can't do.

I know this story may not resonate with everyone on the surface of things, but this story isn't about sexuality. It's about overcoming our biggest fears. It's about seriously examining whatever it is that may be holding us back. I cleared a barrier that at one point felt insurmountable. In fact, for far too long, I allowed myself to believe the self-defeating thought that I'd never overcome it.

All of us have barriers in the way. What's yours? What do you want to do, be, or say, but feel you can't or shouldn't, based on the limitations or expectations within you or those around you? Remember this: your thoughts, wants, needs, and desires are valid. If you keep coming back to a lane in your life that you're too afraid to take, perhaps accept that life is leading you there; maybe one day, try taking it. Get past the fear of the what-if and just do it. Then, and only then, can you know the truth about yourself.

It has taken me a long time to accept who I am and be happy with that person. I regret not doing it sooner. Regret is ignoring a path you should have taken. Don't entertain it. Don't hesitate. I'm gay. I'm living in tune with my best self. And that's what I wish for you: to start living today, not tomorrow.

It Gets Better. Really.

"LIFE'S NOT FAIR! WHY CAN'T things be easy?!"

We've probably all been guilty of thinking, saying, and believing that. But the hardest thing to accept about growing up is this: life, with all its ups and downs, is never going to be a smooth ride, for anyone, of any age.

Question: Why does life have to feel like such a struggle at times?

Answer: Because without the struggle, the triumphs wouldn't taste as sweet. That's why it's important to praise the up parts of life—hold them close and keep them in mind, especially when going through the downs. In my experience, you can't hide from the low periods and merely hope they go away. Instead, you must look them dead in the eye, say, "I've learned from you, but I need to go up now," and begin climbing that hill back to the top. Understanding the rhythm of highs and lows—that one will follow the other and alternate back and forth—can overcome a lot of angst. It's like knowing that after every storm, the sun will shine again. People don't question that truth of Mother Nature, even the ones who live in Seattle. In the same way, we should trust our own nature. Many people first encounter struggle when they are teenagers. The trials and tribulations that coincide with adolescence form the kinds of lessons that teachers don't provide. No one writes on the classroom chalkboard, "Life is going to be hard. Get used to it." In fact, the truest lesson of them all is that our experience of suffering—and, perhaps, our first taste of the blues or depression—begins in high school. Be it heartbreak, bullying, anxiety, stress, or general sadness, we will all graduate from school with a diploma in tough emotions. It is our training ground for that grueling part of life they call adulthood. It's a necessary evil we must go through, and it sucks. It really does.

I experienced real heart-heavy sadness when my inner voice started telling me I'm gay. My attempt to deal with it alone was, in hindsight, not smart, and yet the pain, confusion, and years of absolute hell contained valuable lessons. The very struggle that turned me inside out was also my educator. Here's a quote from Israelmore Ayivor that makes this point for me:

> *Whenever you feel a little stricken down in pain,*
> *think about this: the knife has to be sharpened by*
> *striking and rubbing it against something strong*
> *before it can become useful. You are going to be*
> *great after the struggles!*

Going through any struggle sucks. Going through a struggle *alone* sucks ten times more. My high school years were a struggle in silence. Due to the brave face that I wore, no one could have guessed I was crying myself to sleep some nights, at the mercy of my own thoughts. No one could have guessed the demons I was fighting. I couldn't see

an end in sight. *What is wrong with me? Why do I have to be like this? Will this ever be over?* I asked myself those questions every single day, tormented by the lack of an answer.

By the time I went to college at Saint John's University in Minnesota, all my suppressed sadness, together with low grades throughout my freshman year and not knowing what I wanted to do with my life, led to a slight depression. I needed an out. I wanted to *drop* out. I did eventually, after completing my sophomore year, which turned out to be the right decision for me (though I don't recommend it for everyone). But until that point, I felt wave upon wave of sadness. I didn't want to go out with friends and didn't feel like talking to anyone about anything in case it triggered a sensitive topic.

Nothing aids and abets depression more than being left alone with negative thoughts. That is where a spiral staircase lies, leading to the pit of misery. And I kept going down and down and down, unable to stop. Nothing could make me happy, not even my YouTube career, which began to thrive. Nothing was capable of lifting my spirit. Things felt so gloomy that whenever I found myself doing well, I'd check myself and soon return to bad, negative thoughts. That's what the blues do—they send you in a maddening loop. I could never break the sad cycle for long.

But ultimately I realized that the only person capable of pulling me out of this cycle is me. We each have a choice when feeling down: we become the helpless victim or the self-empowered conqueror. We stay down or get back up. After determining the root cause of my sadness and after admitting to myself and others that I'm gay, the clouds started to part. Once I made an effort to overcome that fear, everything else fell into place. I began to see life through a different lens and went a little easier on myself. Gradually happiness started to take over.

Today, little things make me happy, like going for a walk, getting coffee with a friend, or creating something original. Really, I find happiness in everything now. Having been disoriented for so many years, it's the strangest thing to smile at random times and allow myself to feel good. I had never allowed that before. It's hard to explain, but it feels like I've rediscovered an emotion I had lost, or I've been reunited with a best friend after many years and can't stop grinning. We all go through grim times. But instead of resisting the struggle like I did, embrace it, accept it, and give the matter time to figure itself out. If you trust anything, trust this one fact: nothing lasts for forever. Whatever's bothering you today may not be a problem tomorrow, next week, next month, or even next year. One day, your struggle will be over and you will move on.

So, yes, life has its up and downs. But those who learn to climb out of the downs and reach the ups will prosper. What are you waiting for? Start climbing.

Where I Find Happiness

1. Lying on my back in the middle of an open field with nothing but the stars and moon to feast my eyes on.

2. Relaxing and enjoying a freshly brewed cup of coffee in the morning right after I've gotten up.

3. Lighting a new candle and being completely engulfed in the scent that infuses the room.

4. When my legs first touch the cold sheets while getting into bed.

5. People watching in a busy space. I'm endlessly fascinated by human nature.

6. Deep, personal conversations with a close friend. Talking about anything and everything.

7. Taking a cool photo. Capturing a moment only I see.

8. Creating something; anything, really. The joy is in taking an idea, executing it, and watching it become something.

9. Experiencing something for the first time. Life should be about collecting these firsts.

10. Taking a walk late at night. The streets are empty. Maybe the only sound you hear is a light breeze rustling the leaves. There's room to think and breathe.

11. Making another person laugh or smile. Completely real. Not fake or forced.

12. Traveling to new places and being fully immersed in those surroundings: the food, the people, the culture. I love to collect experiences from around the world.

13. Playing with, petting, holding, or cuddling any cute animal. *Any.* It just has to be cute!

14. Driving with the windows down and the music up. A truly liberating experience.

15. Watching my friends achieve success and do great things. There is a genuine pride and vicarious pleasure that comes from watching your friends do what makes them happy.

16. Waking up hours before you have to, realizing the time, and going back to sleep.

Every day, we should do something that puts a smile on our face or brings us joy.

The Decision That Changed
Everything

U P, DOWN. LEFT AND RIGHT. Diagonal and diagonal again. This was how my sophomore year of college felt—pulled in all directions. While my friends seemed content with where they were headed, I was torn, confused as to which path to take: continuing my education to strengthen my future career prospects or pursuing the opportunities opening up for me on YouTube.

I couldn't have been more frustrated with the dilemma. The classes I was taking were starting to feel lackluster (aside from art class—I loved that one). I was bored to tears and, in the middle of weeping, falling asleep with disinterest. My professors might not have appreciated it, but hey, even with my eyes closed, I was still passing with flying colors, having fully recovered from my rough academic performance freshman year. Crazy what a year can do for you, right? Still, some of the lectures I attended were perfect alternatives to over-the-counter drugs (though way more expensive).

On the face of it, I was doing just fine, though I was clearly losing drive. I was at the halfway point of my college education, pursuing a degree in business, and I hated almost everything. I didn't want to end up working for a corporation like so many college grads before me. I know that sounds ridiculous, considering that's exactly what I signed up for, but, hey, I was young and naive. Don't blame me. Blame someone else!

I had even become disillusioned with athletics—and that had never happened before. *What's the point?* I wondered. *I win a couple competitions, then what? After graduating, what would it all mean anyway?* If it wasn't for the fact I had close friends on both the cross-country and swim teams, I would have thrown in the towel immediately.

I knew where my focus was: the Internet. YouTube, Twitter, Instagram, Tumblr, you name it. I couldn't get my mind off the ever-growing expansion of my social media world, and it started taking over my life, consuming my every thought—and I couldn't have been happier with that.

At night, I'd lie in bed, contemplating the enticing temptation of a YouTube career. Why not let it happen? I saw other YouTubers making it their career. What if I were to follow suit? Place my entire focus on turning a hobby into a pursuit of excellence?

The whole YouTube thing had opened up naturally, and I was starting to make some decent money, to the point where I could justify it as a job in the event of continued growth. But the notion of quitting school for YouTube felt completely insane.

I can't throw away my life for some hobby, I thought. *Who does that?!! People who want to be homeless in three to five years, that's who.*

There just didn't seem to be any longevity in that risky career path.

But hard choices are never easy and nearly always stressful, especially when they affect the trajectory of the rest of your life.

I frequently tear out my hair over the simplest of decisions. The big, life-changing ones require me to talk it out with friends. Like, a lot. I'm always afraid that I'm looking at things too simplistically, without considering the other options. But my instincts were so fierce on this one that I wanted to tell people that I wasn't crazy for thinking what I was thinking. But they didn't get it. And how could they? I barely even got it, and it was happening to me.

I kept talking it out and thinking it through. Months went by when I was almost on autopilot. I felt very robotic in those winter months, doing the bare minimum in the hope that things would figure themselves out. And sure enough, life threw me a bone.

One day, I received a text from Ricky, a YouTube friend. "Connor!! I got accepted to an internship in Los Angeles this summer and my parents said I could go! What if you came with me?"

I stared at the screen and reread the text, letting that invitation

sink in. THIS WAS EXACTLY WHAT I HAD BEEN WAITING FOR—someone could make my decision for me. *insert crying and praise hands emojis here*

I couldn't type my answer quickly enough. "I've gotta ask my parents first, but yes! I'm so down!" I replied.

A long weekend was coming up, so I was going to be home for a couple of days with Mom and Dad. I spent the entire time building up the courage to broach the subject. Then, when I thought they were at their most relaxed and receptive, I announced my plans for a summer vacation.

Surprisingly, they were very okay with it. Maybe it was because my parents are familiar with wanderlust and the need to explore, but they approached it sensibly and pragmatically, eager to ensure that I had thought things through.

"You're going to pay your way to get out there and live?" asked Dad.

"Yup!" I said.

"You'll work hard at your YouTube, keep busy, and stay out of trouble?" asked Mom.

"Definitely!" I said, "And I'll be with Ricky the whole time, so there's no reason to worry."

That did the trick—that, and the fact I had a decent school year nearly under my belt. I was ecstatic. I was going on a road trip across the country to the city where dreams come true—the city where maybe, just maybe, my *own* dreams would come true. Cloud nine had taken me.

I lay down on my bed and allowed my mind to wander, disbelieving that this day had come. You know when you want something so badly but never think it's actually going to happen? The kind of thing that engulfs your mind, the thing that daydreams are made of? This was that thing for me, though I still couldn't define what that "thing" was except,

perhaps, a possible out. And this was my out-of-everything-I-was-doing-but didn't-want to-be-doing. I think I may have even grabbed my pillow and screamed into it with pure excitement that afternoon.

I had no idea what to expect of the adventure I was embarking on. Both the unknowns and the possibilities were endless. All I knew was that I was going to make the best of it. If things went well enough, I'd stay. If they didn't, I'd return. What was the worst that could happen?! I just needed to be smart about this amazing opportunity. *I can take the road to success or the road failure*, I thought. *Both are just as easy. Or hard, depending on your perspective.*

That summer of 2012 was going to be whatever I wanted it to be. But until then, I had to get back to finishing the semester. For the remainder of the school year, I managed to keep up my grades, excel in athletics, and still continue to post weekly on my YouTube channels. I was successfully balancing both worlds, but that success didn't come easily.

There were many long nights, skipped parties, and frustrating conversations that went into making the year go so well. The key was placing my priorities in front of me without letting them control me. With so much on my plate, I couldn't fear potential failure. I had to embrace positive thinking. Sometimes life is going to kick you down, but what matters is how quickly you get back up. The longer you stay in the dirt and complain, the less time you have to brush yourself off and keep moving forward. I had been in the dirt, stagnating, for long enough. I was ready to finally move forward. Things were falling into place and my life's jigsaw puzzle was looking more complete.

I had gone up, down, left, right, and all over the place. Now, I was heading in what felt like the right direction—west, to Los Angeles, California.

Leap of Faith

I WASN'T GOING AWAY FOR A couple of days or weeks. I had a one-way ticket booked. One stop, one destination. No wonder my heart was beating more rapidly than normal when my parents dropped me off at the little airport in La Crosse, Wisconsin. *This is it—the beginning of a journey,* I thought as I waved good-bye to Mom and Dad, like a young child going off to summer camp for the first time.

I vividly remember my parents having last-minute thoughts of allowing me to move away for the summer. "You're. Going. To. DIE!" they kept saying. "Do you have enough money? *How will you make money?* You don't even have a proper education yet!!"

It's fair to say that they were going crazy. I think they both lost it as my departure became imminent. I just shrugged my shoulders. *Oh, well, they already said yes and my ticket is booked.*

As much as I understood their apprehension, I was incredibly excited and not nervous in the slightest. What could go wrong? Nothing. Could I die?? Nah—that doesn't actually happen. (True thoughts from the mind of an invincible teenager.)

I was bound for Florida, of all places, to meet up with my friend and soon-to-be roommate, Ricky Dillon. He and I, both YouTubers, had known each other for maybe a year and were excited to immerse ourselves in the heat of Los Angeles. We had talked about doing something like this from the moment we met, so you can well imagine the levels of our enthusiasm as we began our road trip.

Did I mention that we drove together, for three straight days, across the entire United States, in a car full to the top with everything and anything we could ever need for a summer in LA? No, well, um, minor detail. *coughs awkwardly and walks away*

Details didn't seem to matter. I just wanted to get there. "WE'RE OFF!!" I yelled as we drove away in Ricky's obnoxiously orange, loud Kia Soul. It took three full days to cover the nearly 2,300 miles. Along the way we: stayed in crappy hotels, ate tons of junk food, listened to so much music, talked about life, got lost, picked up our friend Jc Caylen, hit a couple of birds, got pulled over, and ran out of gas and got stranded in the middle of the desert. You know, the usual. But it was an adventure. It's not every day you get to drive all the way across the country. (I highly recommend it if you get the chance. I will never forget that trip.)

The three of us grew dramatically closer on that trip, as you do when spending more than thirty hours in a car. Either that, or you end up wanting to kill each other. Trust me, it happens. It helped that Jc, Ricky, and I were very close in age. Our entire lives revolved around the Internet, and we had just recently begun our collab channel, Our2ndLife, together with our friends Kian Lawley, Sam Pottorff, and Trevor Moran, who conveniently already lived in California.

Basically we all shared one channel, aside from our personal ones, and uploaded six different videos a week revolving around one general theme. I was through-the-roof excited to finally, and permanently, be around like-minded people for a change. These friends truly got me. They had the same interests and ambitions in life. It was refreshing to feel that I didn't have to hold back from being myself around them. With this trip, we were ready to tackle our goals together.

And we did just that individually, but also as O2L, which soon grew to be the biggest collab channel ever on YouTube, with nearly 3 million subscribers. Aside from that, the experience gained me five of the best friends anyone could ask for. But enough of that. Back to this death trap of a road trip!

In its entirety, this shared experience was huge for me. Growing up is full of many little steps, hops, and big leaps, none of them easy. You really can't be totally prepared for any of them. BUT you will always emerge a changed person. Pushing myself to move out of my comfort zone was the best decision I've ever made. Without that move, I wouldn't be where I am today in my career, personal life, and everything in between. Leaving behind the comfort zone forced me to see the real world, away from everything and everyone I know and love. That's a scary thing, but it made me a grown-up, and we all have to do it one day.

Now, I'm not saying you have to move to Los Angeles. I'm saying we all know of potential leaps we could take to make ourselves happy but maybe we avoid them. For a time, I avoided what I wanted by staying in college and doing what everyone else wanted me to do, and I hated it. But as soon as I realized how stagnant I felt, with zero drive, then, and only then, could I initiate change.

I'm young, only a quarter of the way into my life—or less!—with an endless amount of information still to learn, many things to experience, and countless people to meet and places to go. There are many bites to take out of this big wide world, and the opportunities are endless. The only thing holding you back from experiencing them is yourself and the false limitations you've imposed on yourself. Just you. No one else.

Big leaps take time. You don't just wake up one day, have a huge life-altering epiphany, and immediately jump. Well, you could, but it probably wouldn't work out. Or maybe it would. I don't know. I just know that I needed time before translating the idea of something into reality, before being ready for it.

There was endless thinking and planning to be done before I could make the move. And even then, I was never completely prepared to proceed. It's funny now to think about it in retrospect. In fact, how could I be fully ready? How could I prepare myself for the unknown? Sometimes you just have to leap and have faith in yourself.

Moving out and attending college felt difficult.

Moving out and pursuing a career in a different state felt like madness.

But the rewards of doing it outweighed the risks when contemplating it. I headed to LA and placed all my bets on this one trip, believing it would open a new chapter in my life. That was all I could hope for.

Getting to Know Myself

As WE GET OLDER and those ties with our parents, siblings, and close friends from home start to slacken, we begin to better understand the meaning of independence. No longer is it a complaint of "I just want to be left alone." No longer does it mean being shut away behind a closed bedroom door. I'm talking about true on-your-own independence that comes from venturing out into the world all by yourself.

A shiver runs down my spine at the very thought.

The biggest step for me when growing up was when I decided to attend college. At the time, I thought, *YES! I'm finally going to live on my own and be able to do whatever I want!* But a few weeks later, reality dawned: there was no one to do my laundry, cook meals, drive me places, or generally help me with things. *THIS IS DUMB*, I thought. *THIS IS HARD*. I was finally, to be blunt, a real person. *a single tear falls from my eye as I watch the world around me stand completely still*

There were a few phone calls to Mom—okay, they were pretty much daily—but I managed to cope with the change. Eventually I guess we all learn to adjust.

A couple of college years later and as my YouTube channel took off, I was ready to take things to the next level: move out of state and pursue a career. The time had come to leave school behind and move onto bigger and better things in California.

Moving to Los Angeles was terrifying. I didn't have a car. I had never paid my own rent. And due to my mom's cooking and my college's meal plan, I'd barely had to even buy groceries before. Who knew eating could be such a difficult task?! So yeah, I was hesitant about moving to the West Coast. I had no idea what real life was like, what "standing on your own two feet" really meant. Not to mention that I once again had to make new friends, which is never easy. Yes, being alone is tough.

Making friends in school is difficult, but it seems to happen naturally as you share class, lunch, and athletics together. When you move away from all that forced interaction, socializing is completely up to you. There's no written rule that says you can't sit in your crappy apartment all day with no human interaction, going out only to purchase the bare essentials. It's all up to you. The structure and discipline of school and college fall away, requiring you to rebuild your own network.

As you can well assume, I soon made friends. It helped that I moved with Jc and Ricky, who both knew several other people there. But as time went by and I got to know myself—my likes and dislikes, my habits and personality—I realized that I didn't like living with others. I like control over my living space and its cleanliness and supplies (or lack thereof). So, I moved out on my own after sharing an apartment and house with Ricky, Jc, and Kian for nearly a year and a half.

That was when the loneliness set in.

Living alone has many ups and many downs. If there's a mess in

your place, it's on you. If something breaks, it's down to you to fix it and/or pay for the damages. Everything inside the space belongs to you. I know all these things are obvious, but catch my drift? Your life is finally all yours. Nothing and no one is holding you back or cramping your style. It's an extremely liberating feeling.

But then come the downs. There were plenty of nights when I wished I had company—someone in the room next door to sit on the couch with and mindlessly surf through TV channels; someone to walk down the street with and grab a bite to eat; someone to call to pick up milk because "we're out." I lost those simple luxuries when I signed that one-bedroom apartment lease, not to mention that the sense of isolation is ten times worse when you work from home as well. You. Never. Have. To. Leave. EVER!

This new freedom can feel weird at first. Kind of like a new pair of socks—stiff and uncomfortable.

When I realized how alone I truly was, I called my mom, who immediately noticed a slight concern in my voice. "Everything okay?" she asked.

"I'm okay, just a bit lonely," I said. "Like, how do you deal with it?"

"With what, exactly?"

"With being home alone all day by yourself? How do you not go crazy? Who do you hang out with? How do you not feel down from the pure loneliness?"

I accidentally let it all out, as if playing a game of twenty questions. Typical me—jumping right to the chase.

"Oh, honey. I'm kind of glad you get it!" she said. "With all you kids gone and your father at work for most of the day, I feel that way a lot too."

Wait, what?

"It does get a little sad at times," she added, "but I've learned to keep busy! There are always places I can go, people I can see or call, things that need to be done. It's all in your head. You're not really alone—and that feeling is only as strong as you allow it to be."

She spoke so calmly, so matter-of-factly, and then proceeded to update me on what my siblings were up to, how the cats had been, and what local drama was going down. "Can you believe so-and-so is pregnant, and such and such are getting married?!?!"

Oh, small-town folks.

But how right she was to not make a big deal of it. The feeling of loneliness is temporary. It can easily be replaced by another feeling or action. Now, when I'm feeling down, I pick up the phone and call a friend for a chat or to meet. How can you be lonely if there is always someone to reach out to or spend time with? Loneliness really is a state of mind.

When living alone with only thoughts for company, it's all too easy to allow them to fill the void and take you over. Now I totally understand that taming your thoughts can be difficult. It's easy to get in your head and make the situation worse than it actually is (trust me; I'm there quite a lot). But Mom's right—a thought is only as strong as you allow it to be. We either fuel it or release it. Same with loneliness.

I do wonder how many people avoid alone time because of the thoughts and silence they have to sit with, and I get it: living by yourself can be scary, but what big decision isn't? Get past the fear and view it as an opportunity. You'll be all the stronger for it. Being alone is a chance to really get to know yourself, in isolation from the influence and chatter of others. Take a breath. Take a chance. Move on and move out. You've got this.

The Myth of "Fame"

Scenario One: LOS ANGELES, 9:14 a.m. We'll say it's a Thursday. I wake up, sit at the table with my computer for a bit, then decide to go for a quick walk to the nearby Starbucks. Everything is quiet. No one sees me. No one knows me.

I'm just a regular guy.

Scenario Two: ORLANDO, 9:14 a.m. We'll say it's Playlist Live. I wake up in my hotel room, sit in bed with my computer for a bit, then decide to go for a little walk to Starbucks. Everything is quiet. From behind me, I hear screams. I turn around. Several hundred teenagers are hurrying toward me, yelling my name. It's a STAMPEDE. Suddenly everyone seems to know who I am.

Welcome to my topsy-turvy world, one that I'm still getting used to. When I began this journey four years ago, sitting in a bedroom talking into a camera, it never crossed my mind that I'd ever become well known. Never in a million years did I think that this form of fame would hit me like a high-speed train. Someone like me doesn't seek to be "famous." In fact, it was probably the polar opposite of what I aspired to be. And yet it's become a by-product of the career I've pursued. How ironic that the boy who never particularly enjoyed attention is now getting a whole lot of it as a consequence of doing what he loves.

Before I dive in any further, I would like to make clear how uneasy the word *famous* makes me. It is, after all, just another misleading label. Unfortunately, there is a negative connotation with this word, and I understand why. For me, it has something pretentious and distasteful about it. "What's it like being famous?" is a question I get all the time, and it embarrasses me because I don't consider myself "famous" at all.

I would prefer the focus to be trained on the quality of work I produce rather than the number of people viewing it. I prefer saying that I have more than 4 million people interested in my posts than say I have 4 million fans. I'm just someone who happens to be creating content for the enjoyment of others to fill the creative void within me. But getting recognized and receiving messages and tweets from people all around the world comes with this new territory. It's something I've had to adjust to, because although this shift didn't magically happen overnight, it did happen extremely, and semiuncomfortably, quickly.

I don't think I had properly grasped the reality of how much my YouTube hobby was beginning to take off when I was still in college. Maybe the remoteness of Minnesota had shielded me somewhat, but after moving to Los Angeles, I noticed people noticing me. As the weeks went on, I started getting stopped on the street, in restaurants, and in shopping malls and began getting attention from businesses, events, parties, and award shows in the entertainment industry. My manager said I had "gone mainstream" and, yeah, that made me laugh. But suddenly a number on a screen—YouTube subscribers or Twitter followers—had mutated into real, living, breathing human beings. (When I put it that way, it sounds like some weird, twisted horror film!) Those clicks weren't all made by some freak accident. All those strangers were out there and knew me—and I needed to wrap my head around this new normal, however strange it felt.

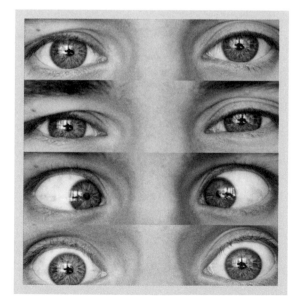

Life got even stranger at the MTV Video Music Awards in 2014 when I found myself standing in the middle of a Taylor Swift, Miley Cyrus, Adam Levine triangle on the red carpet. That was a crazy experience, and thank God I'm not the type to freak out over celebrities; otherwise I would have been an utter mess—crying and asking for selfies in between sobs. But it was truly a cool moment for me, and not something I had anticipated at the start of the day.

I had woken early, probably because of the butterflies fluttering in my stomach, and thought, *Today's the day! Award show day!*

In true Connor Franta fashion, I had purchased my outfit the day before: a gray blazer, nice white button-down with a unique black stripe down the middle, black pants, and my fancy, shiny shoes ta boot! Or, um, ta shoe! I looked good. I felt good.

My car pulled up, and I stepped outside into the California heat. During the forty-five-minute journey through traffic, my mind started to wander . . . and reflect . . . and take stock as my thoughts raced back to La Crescent and those days attending a tiny college in Collegeville, Minnesota. And now, here I was in a fancy black car, on my way to a nationally televised award show, produced by MTV— and they had invited me; they wanted me there. I didn't have to ask, beg, or even grovel. I pinched myself. That was definitely the moment when I knew the risk—the move out West—had paid off. After many difficult decisions, wide-eyed nights, and careful thinking, I had made it to a place I never thought possible. Living the life and chasing the career I never knew would turn into this.

When the car arrived at the award show, I snapped out of my reflective daydream and was shepherded through the glitzy hustle and bustle toward the red carpet. There, I was greeted by the sound of scream after scream—"CONNNORRRR!!"—and the mad flutter of paparazzi camera shutters. Incredible.

I pinched myself again.

"Ow!" I winced. *Why did I do that?*

Everything I've been through and built up to goes far beyond this award show or the "fame" associated with it. I was there in recognition of my work—and that was the reward. I'm just happy that the things I'm doing and creating mean something to my audience. In fact, I shouldn't even be saying "I" when it's more a "we." We, the YouTube community, have always dreamed of receiving such plaudits. That night at the VMAs, I looked around and saw many of my peers paired with mainstream celebrities and felt nothing but pride.

It's happening, and quickly. And it's going to get bigger. I'm ready for this ride we're all on. Let's push the limits and show the world we mean business. Time to hop on that high-speed train.

Charity

I grew up volunteering my time at local nursing homes, church, food shelters, and my community in general. My parents always encouraged us to think of the plight of others, so I was no stranger to charity. But I always walked away thinking that I'd like to do much more beyond just giving my time.

Ever since my YouTube channel started to grow, I have wanted to get directly involved with a charity of some sort, but I could never put a finger on which one. The world is filled with things that need fixing and people who need our love, so how do you simply pick one? That's a tough choice to make, but I made it in August 2014.

One evening, while scouring the Internet for who knows what, I stumbled on The Thirst Project. In a nutshell, this organization provides safe drinking water to people in Africa, with local residents hired to build wells in villages, thus stimulating the economy. What really hooked me—aside from its founder Seth Maxwell's passion for the cause—was the understanding that water was only the start of many issues that villagers faced. If these people didn't first have to walk all day to obtain water from a dirty stream, they could be working and their children could be getting an education. If they were able to drink safe water, they were less likely to get sick from a contaminated source. Fix the water problem; fix them all. Amazing.

After quickly bringing together a launch page and a game plan, I began a fundraising campaign using YouTube videos, tweets, and other social media one month later, on September 12, 2014, my birthday. The response blew me away. Within the next thirty days, my followers and I had raised more than $230,000.

All it takes to make a difference is an idea, a little initiative, and the determination to make it happen. I realized that I could use my influence—and large audience—to do good in one needy corner of the world. After what we achieved, I have never been prouder of my audience or myself. Giving back is a real blessing. Charity is where the heart is, and it asks us to put our personal needs, wants, and desires aside for a bit and instead place them in the hands of people less fortunate. As Mother Teresa put it, "It's not how much we give but how much love we put into giving."

From the bottom of my heart, thank you to anyone and everyone who contributed. We did a good thing.

Life Doesn't Wait

D O YOU KNOW what's a strange feeling? Beginning to write a book.
Do you know what's an even stranger feeling? Finishing a book.

I seriously cannot believe I've made it this far—from blank page to finish line! What's interesting is that I've never before worked for this amount of time—nearly one year now—on a project. I'm more used to thinking something up, creating it, and immediately sharing it with the world. So to craft, nurture, and sit with a project for so long without sharing it with anyone has been a test. A test of patience, drive, creativity, and, frankly, writing abilities.

To the five of you who have taken the time to sit down and read my book cover to cover, thank you. I hope you feel as if you've been taken on a journey of self-discovery while learning a bit more about me and the way I see the world. This world is a strange place in reality, and even stranger from my point of view.

We all have many chapters left to live, but here I am, on the final pages of this installment. So how should this book end? I've thought long and hard about this. Isn't the ending supposed to be the best part? The part that sticks with people the most? The part that can make or break a story? That's a lot of pressure! I may be getting a minor anxiety attack right now from merely typing about it.

Breathe, Connor. Breathe.

Okay. I've got it. Let's wrap with the best advice I can give anyone.

Life waits for no one. Are you happy with where you are and what you're doing? If you have to search yourself for an answer to that simple question, you probably aren't. It's not okay to just get by, *existing* day to day. Where will that get you? Aren't we here to *live?* To squeeze the maximum amount of juice out of life and, at the end of the day, say to ourselves, *Wow, I'm so grateful to have what I have, and do what I do. I'm the luckiest person on the planet.*

I once overheard a friend talking about his aunt who works a 9-to-5 job, doing the same thing over and over again, every day. In her late forties, she's been doing her mundane job for ten years, a sort of professional Groundhog Day. Now, there is absolutely no problem with working pretty much any job for any number of hours if you love it. But therein lies the problem with this person: she hates her job. "But there's no way out," my friend said. "She's trapped by the necessity to work to earn an income in order to survive."

My heart sank for her as I listened to that story. If you ask me, she might as well be in prison. Routine becomes the confining walls of a prison if you don't take comfort in it. And yet that idea of a robotic life, in which there is nothing left to excite or motivate you, potentially awaits us all if we surrender to either the easiest options or the expectations others have for us that we don't share for ourselves.

Why put yourself through that? Don't give up that easily.

Don't allow yourself to settle for just anything in your life.

Strive to obtain your every want and desire, as long as you're not harming others.

I say this as someone who felt imprisoned within himself. I was there, but I got out of it relatively quickly. I had ambition. I had dreams. And I had to pursue them; otherwise my soul would have shriveled. The hardest part was allowing myself to want something other than what was socially acceptable, telling myself to go after it, then actually doing it.

Actually doing what you want can be the most difficult thing. Yes, the risk was huge and it could have all blown up in my face, but I couldn't live with the what-if—the answer to: "What if I don't try?"

What have you got to lose?

My favorite YouTube video I ever made was about this topic, and I'd like to share the raw text with you, bare for all to see.

As the title says, "Life Doesn't Wait."

I'm tired, I'm so tired
not from a lack of sleep
but from a sheer amount of disbelief
from seeing the watercolor world we live in
slowly turning a light shade of tin
smiles fade to frowns
ups turn to downs
some of us have lost that spark
lost our drive
lost our heart
and frankly, I'm tired of it
I'm exhausted by the sight
of lives lacking a certain light
when each & every one of us deserve that right?
Now do me a favor & lend me your ears
keep your eyes peeled, place them here
Poetry and fancy wordplay on hold,
Here's a meaningful story I've never told:

A couple of weeks ago, on a day like any other,
I was heading out to meet up with some friends
for lunch. For some reason, I couldn't be bothered
to tackle the mess that is Los Angeles parking,
so I called a taxi. After a couple of minutes of
waiting, I saw the car approaching and left my
apartment and met this yellow vehicle at the curb.
I'm the type of person who likes to make
conversation with pretty much anyone and everyone,
whether it's an old lady at a bus stop or a barista

at a coffee shop. People are people and they all have something to say; everyone has a unique story to tell. After a few introductory sentences, this thirty-something gentleman realized we were both creative types, originally from the Midwest, living in Los Angeles, pursuing our many artsy endeavors.

We continued conversing and things got deeper quickly. He asked me, "Was your family okay with you moving to a bigger city and chasing such an alternative type of career?"

"Definitely!" I said. "They're just happy that I'm happy, doing something I love every day."

He continued by saying, "Good, that's really good that you're doing something you're passionate about. A lot of people nowadays can't say that." And then he added: "You know, my dad and brother worked night and day for practically their entire lives, receiving little pay, doing something they didn't enjoy at all. They both always talked about how it'll be worth it one day! 'We can spend our hard earned money later on! We will live a good life eventually.' But you know what? Neither of them ever got that. My dad died unexpectedly four years ago and my brother, just last year. They'll never get to live that life they always wanted to, so it's nice to see other people following their hearts and living their lives now, rather than later."

And that's when he dropped me off.

After only a 10-minute car ride
I left with a new perspective in my mind
life waits for no one.
if yours isn't going the way you want it to
if you aren't pursuing what you want to
    pursue
if you wake up with immediate dread
constantly saddened by the hours ahead
moving through the days
feeling lost, heart in a haze
holding back what you want to say
waiting to be yourself another day
your dreams & desires put on hold
to be fulfilled, maybe when you're old
you aren't doing it right
you aren't living your life
eventually is not okay
why tomorrow when there is today?

I finally feel like I'm finding my way
and not just living day by day
I'm doing what I love
I'm going where I want to go
I'm being who I want to be
I'm happy

And you know what? I think everyone deserves
to feel the same way.

• • •

I'm just a small-town kid trying to find my place in the world. I've only been around for twenty-two years and there's so much left for me to explore and learn. I've been through an incredible amount already, but there are more ups and downs to come. I don't know when or where, but that uncertainty is a beautiful thing. All I know is that I need to keep moving forward in the direction I'm happy with.

I refuse to live a life of regret. I refuse to hope things will get better in the future when I have complete control over making them the best possible right here and now. We have one life—and none of us knows how long our life will be or what will become of it. The possibilities are truly infinite.

The future is as bright as you let it shine. Don't be tricked into seeing it dimly. Don't be fooled into believing that this, where you are right now, is all you get. Your potential is endless. Just act. Act now. Right now. Leap. Live. Love.

So what are you waiting for? Go. Get started.

Acknowledgments

To my editors, Jhanteigh and Steve: Thank you for dealing with my constant e-mails, many phone calls, desperate meetings, and giving me the general help I needed to complete this huge project. I couldn't have done it without your patience and counsel.

To my manager, Andrew: Thank you for guiding me through this, as well as all of my entrepreneurial endeavors. Without your positive push, I wouldn't have had the courage to even begin this book.

To my creative consultant and best friend, Troye: Thank you for all the ingenious input you give to me on all of my creations. I appreciate you and trust your eye more than anyone else's.

To my friends back home, Alli, Jacob, Douglas, Kirstin, Kayla, Brooke, Stephanie, and Emilie: Thank you for living the most memorable moments of my childhood with me. I wouldn't trade those long hours in the pool with you all for the world.

To my family, Dad, Mom, Dustin, Nicola, and Brandon: Thank you for your endless love and support. I can't begin to describe how acknowledgments

proud I am to come from a family as amazing as ours. I love you all with every inch of my being.

Last but surely not least, to you, the reader: Whether this is the first or millionth time you've heard of me, thank you. The amount of support I receive on a daily basis is heartwarming, and I wouldn't be where I am today without it. You're a special bunch and are going to do great things in the world. I feel truly blessed to have you on this journey with me.